D1759587

Books are to be returned on or before
the last date below.

The political theory of animal rights

MANCHESTER
1824
Manchester University Press

PERSPECTIVES ON DEMOCRATIZATION

The series presents critical texts on democratization processes and democratic theory. Written in an accessible style, the books are theoretically informed and empirically rich, and examine issues critical to the establishment, extension and deepening of democracy in different political systems and contexts. Important examples of successful democratization processes, as well as reasons why experiments in democratic government fail, are some of the issues analysed in the series. The books in the series make an important contribution to the ongoing debates about democracy, good governance and democratization.

SHIRIN M. RAI AND WYN GRANT   series editors

already published

Democracy as public deliberation
MAURIZIO PASSERIN D'ENTRÈVES   (editor)

Terrorism and democratic stability
JENNIFER S. HOLMES

Democratizing the European Union
CATHERINE HOSKYNS AND MICHAEL NEWMAN   (editors)

Democracy in Latin America
GERALDINE LIEVESLEY

Mainstreaming gender, democratizing the state?
SHIRIN RAI   (editor)

Trade unions and democracy
GEOFFREY WOOD AND MARK HARCOURT   (editors)

The political theory of animal rights

ROBERT GARNER

MANCHESTER UNIVERSITY PRESS
Manchester and New York

distributed exclusively in the USA by Palgrave

Published by Manchester University Press
Oxford Road, Manchester M13 9NR, UK
and Room 400, 175 Fifth Avenue, New York, NY 10010, USA
www.manchesteruniversitypress.co.uk

Distributed exclusively in the USA by
Palgrave, 175 Fifth Avenue, New York,
NY 10010, USA

Distributed exclusively in Canada by
UBC Press, University of British Columbia, 2029 West Mall,
Vancouver, BC, Canada V6T 1Z2

British Library Cataloguing-in-Publication Data
A catalogue record for this book is available from the British Library

Library of Congress Cataloging-in-Publication Data applied for

ISBN 0 7190 6710 3 hardback
EAN 978 0 7190 6710 5

First published 2005

14 13 12 11 10 09 08 07 06 05   10 9 8 7 6 5 4 3 2 1

Typeset in Trump Medieval
by Graphicraft Limited, Hong Kong
Printed in Great Britain
by Bell & Bain Ltd, Glasgow

Contents

Preface

Although this book was conceived some five years ago, it is the culmination of many more years of study and writing about the issue of the moral status of nonhuman animals. As such, it incorporates some material that originally appeared in journal articles. Two articles have been drawn from in various places in this book; 'Animal Rights, Political Theory and the Liberal Tradition' appeared in *Contemporary Politics* (8, 1, 2002: 7–22) and 'Political Ideologies and the Moral Status of Animals' appeared in the *Journal of Political Ideologies* (8, 2, 2003: 233–46). The website of the former journal is www.tandf.co.uk/journals/carfax/13569775.html and the latter www.tandf.co.uk/journals/carfax 13569317. html. Chapter 2 is an expanded version of an article originally published as 'Political Ideology and the Legal Status of Animals' in the journal *Animal Law* (8, 2002: 77–91). Chapter 3, likewise, is a much embellished version of an article 'Animals, Politics and Justice: Rawlsian Liberalism and the Plight of Non-humans' that was published in *Environmental Politics* (12, 2, 2003: 3–22). Chapter 5 contains some material from 'Animal Protection and Legislators in Britain and the United States', published in the *Journal of Legislative Studies* (5, 2, 1999: 92–114) and chapter 6 some material from 'Wildlife Conservation and the Moral Status of Animals', published in *Environmental Politics* (3, 1, 1994: 114–29).

I have benefited enormously from, mostly anonymous, referees' reports on the articles referred to above, as well as rather more transparent comments from critics in response to the expression of my ideas in papers given in seminars and at conferences. I am also grateful to my institution, the University of Leicester, which has provided two study leaves, separated by three years, which enabled me to be free of teaching and administration during crucial points of the research and writing process. I would also like to thank Andy Dobson for his general support and encouragement and, more specifically, for making some typically incisive criticisms of the first draft of this book.

My son, Keir, was born in the early stages of preparing this book. Whilst it would be inaccurate to claim that he has speeded up its progress, his presence has been a joy and made, with apologies to Tony Mason and the good folk at MUP, submission deadlines seem slightly less relevant!

Introduction: the political representation of nonhuman interests

This is not another book outlining the case for animal rights or liberation. Or at least it is not only, or primarily, concerned with this objective. A relatively brief part of the text is concerned with setting out the case for an enhanced moral status for nonhuman animals and the reader is advised to look elsewhere for a more comprehensive account.[1] A much greater part of this book is concerned with exploring the relationship between the moral status of animals and political thinking in general. Indeed, the two main tasks of the book are to ask what is the most appropriate ideological location for protecting animal interests, and, secondly, what impact does an expanded moral status for animals have on political concepts and political ideologies in general? In the process of completing these tasks this book will also cover some of the major issues in contemporary political theory, not least the debates between advocates of liberalism and communitarianism; rights, utility and contractariansm; neutral and perfectionist theories of the state and liberal and feminist theories of justice.

Academics have played an important role in both the women's movement and the civil rights movement, and the political science literature has been affected significantly by their work. The animal rights or liberation movement, by contrast, has made fewer political, social and academic advances. It is true that animal welfare has become an intermittently important issue in some countries, and particularly Britain. It is true too that some academics, from a wide variety of disciplines, have devoted at least some of their time to a consideration of, for instance, the philosophical, psychological and theological relationships between humans and animals. Given the obvious political saliency of the animals issue it is surprising then that the human/animal relationship has been virtually ignored by the political studies community. In particular, the absence of a comprehensive account of the potential implications for political theory of granting to animals an elevated moral status is an important blind spot in the discipline. If a strong case for an elevated moral status for animals is established, this has important consequences for political theory, just as feminism has had important consequences for the conceptualization of political concepts such as the state, freedom, power justice and so on (Squires, 1999).

Ecocentrism, anthropocentrism and animal welfare

Democracy is, first and foremost, concerned with the representation of interests. The question of whether, and to what degree, the interests of nonhumans should be represented in the political process is an important one. Nonhuman interests include non-sentient parts of nature as well as nonhuman animals. There is a debate within the discipline of Green political thought about the most effective way of representing the interests of nature. Traditionally, one characteristic of a radical Green approach has been the adoption of an ecocentric ethic, whereby the whole of nature is accorded intrinsic value (see Fox, 1995; Johnson, 1991; Naess, 1973). Despoiling nature, then, matters to nature itself and can be morally prohibited on the grounds that it damages its interests. More recently, a number of academics have sought to re-emphasize that it is possible, and more politically acceptable, to defend nature by invoking an anthropocentric, or human-centred, ethic (J. Barry, 1999: chapters 2 and 3; Dobson, 2000; Hayward, 1995 and 1998; Norton, 1991; Vincent, 1993: 254–5). This so-called 'enlightened anthropocentrism' view holds that it can be shown that protecting the interests of nature is in the interests of humans too and it is therefore superfluous to seek to defend the intrinsic value of nonhuman nature.

Whether or not such a claim can be upheld is disputed (see Garner, 2000). What is clear is that the dichotomy described above – between an ecocentric and an anthropo-centric ethic – neglects the fact that the philosophical, social and political consensus, at least in the developed world, is that what we do to nonhuman animals matters to them and as a result we have direct duties towards them. An important distinction, used throughout this book, is that between moral standing and moral significance. Following Goodpaster (1978) I take the former to mean the existence of *any* degree of direct moral considerability, the latter to mean the *degree* of moral worth, so that, as Attfield (2003: 43) clarifies, 'moral standing ... is compatible with different degrees of moral significance'. Few radical Greens adopting an ecocentric ethic are prepared to argue that all parts of nature have equal moral status, although all insist that non-sentient parts of nature have moral standing. Likewise, arguing that we have direct duties to animals does not mean that humans and animals should be regarded as morally equivalent. In the West at least, it is – with few exceptions – the ideological norm to accept that animals have at least some moral worth, that what we do to them matters to them and ought to be guided by some kind of moral framework. The acceptance of this – animal welfare position or the moral orthodoxy – which, as is shown below, regards humans as morally superior to animals but not all-conquering, dents anthropocentrism, because on occa-sions the interests of animals might outweigh the interests of humans. Enhancing the moral status of animals further, to a point where the moral claims of humans and animals are equivalent, sends it to the scrap yard.

The choice to focus on nonhuman animals in this book and to exclude for the most part the claims of nature as a whole is based partly on limitations of space, but also on grounds of intellectual conviction – there is a strong case, as the discussion in chapter 6 suggests, for enhancing the moral status of animals, less of one for the intrinsic value of non-sentient parts of nature. Political saliency is an important factor too. The animal protection movement has grown sig-nificantly in recent years in many countries and on both sides of the Atlantic (Finsen and Finsen, 1994; Garner, 1993; Jasper and Nelkin, 1992). This growth is not at all surprising if one considers the huge gulf between the demands of the animal rights movement and the present scale of animal ex-ploitation by humans.

Animals are used for a wide variety of human purposes: as a source of food, clothing and entertainment; as models for human diseases; as testers for products humans use; as aids, in the case of companion animals, for human psychological health and, particularly in the case of majestic wild animals, aesthetic pleasure. The bottom line is that the exploitation of animals is the source of a great deal of economic benefit. In the United States, for instance, the meat and poultry industries, second only to cars as the biggest manufacturing and processing concern, generate an income of $90 billion a year (Mason, 2002: 201). Similarly, the trade in animals, dead and alive, is now the third biggest illegal trade after arms and drugs, estimated to be worth between $5 and $20 billion a year (Roberts, 2002: 45).

The scale of this exploitation is almost too immense to fathom. In the United States alone, some 103 million pigs and 38 million cows and calves are slaughtered each year. Worldwide, eight million pigs are slaughtered *every day* (Scully, 2002: 30, 284). As many as 800 million broiler chickens – the vast majority of which are raised and fattened for as little as six weeks before slaughter in very intensive indoor conditions – are produced each year in Britain alone whilst the figure for the United States is three billion (Mason and Singer, 1990: 8). As Scully (2002: 30) concludes, this is 'an awful lot of killing. You would think such figures would make a man draw back, question a premise or two and ask where it all leads.' This book is one of many that attempts to raise concerns about the treatment of animals and, to my knowledge, the only one which examines the impact on political thinking of treating them better than we currently do.

The degree to which the interests of animals are represented in the political process can be measured empirically. In both Britain and America, for instance, there is now an extensive legislative and administrative framework designed to protect at least some interests of animals (Garner, 1998). This structure has been created as a result of the acceptance of a moral consensus by civil society and governments in most developed countries. This moral consensus, both philosophical and political, is centred on the notion of animal welfare. This position holds that animals have intrinsic value, that what is done to them matters to them, but that their interests should be regarded as less important than those of humans. As a result, animal interests will always be sacrificed in the event of a clash with the significant interests of humans. However, prohibiting unnecessary suffering – suffering which serves no significant human purpose – is a moral obligation from the perspective of animal welfare, and the widespread adoption of animal welfare has resulted in the protection of some animal interests, and their representation in the political and legal processes of many countries.

What is regarded as 'unnecessary' suffering, of course, is a matter of political debate and is intimately related to what is regarded as a 'significant' human interest. Changing human priorities and levels of knowledge over the years has resulted in greater protection for animal interests. Thirty years ago, for instance, there was little opposition to the toxicity testing of cosmetic products, the wearing of fur or the keeping of farm animals in industrialized 'factory' farms. Now, in Britain and elsewhere, there is widespread criticism of such practices. As a result, there are cases, such as, for instance, the banning of fur farms and veal crates in Britain, where what previously might have been regarded as significant human interests have been sacrificed in order to protect some animal interests.

The protection afforded by animal welfare, however, is very fragile. At any time the interests of humans can be invoked and, as a result, the most fundamental interests of animals may be sacrificed. According to animal welfare it is not just what is done to an animal that determines the moral parameters, but also the *purpose* of what is done. Burning, poisoning and shooting an animal will result in legal sanctions if done for fun but will be permitted and, indeed, licensed by the state if conducted as part of a scientific project that can be shown to have likely and significant human benefits. Likewise, under British law, keeping a bird as a pet in a cage so small that it cannot spread its wings is illegal, yet keeping a hen in such a condition in a battery cage is, for the time being at least, entirely permissible on the grounds that economic benefits to both consumers and producers are said to accrue.

Despite its practical importance in defending some animal interests, the animal welfare concept offers no real challenge to conventional political thinking. Animals are not regarded as being morally equivalent to humans, and therefore the concept of equality can remain anthropocentric. Likewise, animals remain the property of humans, are not regarded as rights holders, or significant enough to be granted legal standing, or have their interests represented in the political process on a par with humans. Above all, the humane killing of an animal, for whatever purpose, does not trouble the moral conscience of an animal welfarist who is only concerned about the pain and suffering of an animal whilst alive. In other words, the most fundamental interest of an animal – staying alive – is not protected at all, under any circumstances, by animal welfare.[2] By contrast, if we accept the case for increasing the moral status of animals then more profound implications would seem to follow. It is these implications that this book is primarily concerned about.

Animals, liberalism and beyond

Much philosophical attention in the past thirty years or so has been directed at the moral status of animals. With some notable exceptions (see Carruthers, 1992; Leahy, 1991; Scruton, 2000; Tester, 1991), the bulk of this literature has been concerned with justifying a case for a higher moral status for animals than the animal welfare approach allows. It is a little-commented, but hardly surprising, fact that most of these accounts are written from within the liberal tradition. As Benton (1993a: 161) elaborates:

> The most influential advocates of an improved moral status for animals have taken their stand *with* the prevailing moral discourses, and attempted to show that they cannot consistently be confined within the species boundary.

Given its importance, the first three chapters of this book are devoted to an exploration of this liberal dimension.

The first chapter documents the absence of concern for animals in much mainstream liberal political theory, both historically and contemporaneously, and outlines the pro-animal liberal responses from thinkers writing from rights, utilitarian and contractarian positions. The first two of these challenges – associated above all, but by no means exclusively, with the work of Regan (1984) and Singer (1990) respectively – are perhaps better known than the third. This consists largely of an attempt to revise Rawls (1972) by including animals as entities who can be the beneficiaries of the deliberations in the original position, a philosophical device designed to generate more or less objective principles of justice to which everyone can assent. It is contended that this revision of Rawls – associated, above all, with Rowlands (1998), does not offer, as is claimed, a superior grounding for a higher moral status for animals than the more traditional rights and utilitarian approaches.

It is a major contention of this book that the protection of animals from within the liberal paradigm is problematic. It is important to see initially what is *not* problematic. The problem with liberalism does not stem, in this author's view at any rate, from the granting of rights to animals or their inclusion within a non-speciesist utilitarian calculus. If successfully achieved, then animals are on a par with humans subject, along with humans, only to the limitations of these competing ethical viewpoints. Nor does the problem stem from the fact that animals, if denied rights, are regarded as the property of humans. As chapter 2 will show, whilst it is true that the equal consideration of human and animal interests cannot be achieved unless the property status of the latter is removed, regarding animals as property is not in practice, despite assertions to the contrary (see Francione, 1995), a barrier to a relatively high level of protection for animals.

The major problem with liberalism is that it is unlikely, for the reasons explored in chapter 2, that animals will sometime soon be granted a moral status equivalent to humans or anything like it. This leaves them vulnerable, as chapter 3 suggests, to the implications of the central liberal concept of moral pluralism, upheld by leading liberal political theorists such as Barry (1995), Dworkin (1978) and Rawls (1972). Taken to its logical extreme, this principle holds that the state should not contemplate interfering with individual moral codes or conceptions of the good life – including those involving animals – until actions deriving from them seem likely to harm other humans in a direct way. The way in which we treat animals, therefore, becomes a moral preference rather than an obligation insisted upon by the state. Rawls and others clearly do not want to hold the view that we are morally entitled to do whatever we like to animals. On the other hand, if they seek to constrain the way in which we treat animals, they are placing limits upon moral pluralism. It is argued in this book that only by incorporating animals within a theory of justice, which leading liberal political theorists such as Rawls have refused to do, can liberalism be rescued. Moreover, in practice, irrespective of the degree to which liberal political theorists do want to limit moral pluralism, the principle has been utilized in the animal welfare debate – most notably by those seeking to defend hunting and the ritual slaughter of animals – to justify the exploitation of animals.

To repeat, the problem with liberalism is not that it is intellectually unable to incorporate the interests of animals as more or less equivalent to humans, but that such an outcome is politically unlikely and, as a result, animals are vulnerable to exclusion. To a certain extent, this is a problem of agency. As Benton (1993a: 161) remarks, while the strategy of seeking to incorporate animal interests within the dominant ideology:

> has been relatively effective in getting the moral status of animals onto the agenda of 'established' moral philosophy . . . it has had the consequence of detaching animal rights advocacy from potential allies among the radical critics of the established moral discourses and practices.

Because of the problematic relationship between liberalism and the protection of animals, the rest of this book, chapters 4–7, is concerned with assessing the validity of alternative ideological locations for animal protection, where the allies Benton refers to may be found.[3] Chapter 4 examines the claims of communitarianism and conservatism, chapter 5 explores the relationship between animals and the left, and chapters 6 and 7 focus on ecology and feminism respectively.

Following the analysis of the political theory of animal rights in this book two main themes are identified. Firstly, whilst there are a number of problems with deriving a viable ethic for the treatment of animals from within a liberal perspective, no other ideological position appears to offer a better alternative, although there may be features derived from them that can improve liberalism's ability to incorporate the interests of animals. Secondly, after reviewing the literature linking competing political ideologies with animal protection, it is suggested that the acceptance of a substantial degree of moral status for animals – which adopts the view that their interests ought to be considered on a par with humans, or close to it – does not necessarily challenge the conceptual morphology of political theory but, by decentring humans as the major beneficiaries and 'expanding the circle' (Singer, 1981) to include animals as morally worthy beings, it has a profound effect on the distribution of benefits deriving from political principles.

Notes

1 The classic texts are Clark (1984); Midgley (1983); Regan (1984); and Singer (1990). Introductory accounts of the arguments are provided by DeGrazia (1996 and 2002) and Garner (1993). Rowlands (2002) offers an extremely well-written and accessible introduction and Francione (2000) is also worth reading, although offering a more idiosyncratic text. Pluhar (1995) focuses on one particular argument in the debate.

2 The lives of members of endangered species are sometimes protected even if some human interests are harmed in the process. This is usually undertaken for anthropocentric reasons, though, so that the conflict is between competing human interests rather than between human and animal interests (see chapter 6).

3 This coverage is by no means exhaustive. There is no mention, for instance, of non-Western belief systems such as Buddhism and Hinduism, both of which have interesting things to say about the relationship between humans and animals, but which ought probably to be the subject matter of an entirely different book.

1

Animal interests, political theory and the liberal tradition

This chapter charts the position of animals within liberal thought. Mainstream political theory in general, and exponents of liberal thought in particular, has been unwilling to incorporate the interests of nonhuman animals. It was common amongst pre-nineteenth-century political thinkers to exclude animals completely as beings with interests, and therefore moral standing. Since the nineteenth century it has become the norm to accept that animals do have moral standing, but that the interests of humans must take precedence on the grounds that we have a level of rationality that, among other things, allows us to be moral agents. Many of the key names in contemporary liberal political theory – most notably John Rawls – while accepting that animals have some moral worth, still insist that they are not morally significant enough to be included, along with humans, as recipients of justice.

Despite the consistent devaluing of animal interests from within the liberal tradition, it is nevertheless the case that the most sustained, and best known, attempts to justify a higher moral status for animals than the moral orthodox allows has come from thinkers operating from within this very tradition. The process of philosophically challenging the moral orthodoxy can be divided into two phases. In the first, it is necessary to critically examine and overturn the arguments employed for granting humans a higher moral status than animals. In particular, this involves either denying that animals lack the autonomy or personhood said to be crucial in determining moral status, or denying that autonomy or personhood is the best determinant of moral status. In the second, it is necessary to consider what is the best theoretical framework for protecting the interests of humans and the equivalently valued interests of animals. This involves considering the relative methods of a rights-based approach – associated with Tom Regan (1984), among others – and a utilitarian-based approach, associated with Peter Singer (1990). Another approach that can be used to stride the two phases is the contractarian approach, which typically consists of an attempt to revise Rawls by incorporating animals as the beneficiaries, along with humans, of the deliberations in the original position. While there is a good case for saying that animals ought to be so incorporated, this chapter will also suggest that Rawls' contractarianism does not offer, as is claimed, a superior grounding for a higher moral status for animals than the more traditional rights and utilitarian approaches.

Animals and moral standing

Moral and political philosophers have regularly considered the status of animals. Three main positions have emerged. Animals either have no moral standing, moral standing but with a level of moral significance inferior to that of humans, or moral significance more or less equivalent to that of humans. These positions, and their adherents, can be described as follows:
1. Completely lacking moral status. Only indirect duties owed to animals.
   (a) Animals lack sentiency (Descartes, Carruthers).
   (b) Animals are sentient but lack any morally significant interests (Kant, Frey).
2. Moral orthodoxy/Animal welfare/Humane treatment – some moral status but inferior to humans.
   (a) Animals have an interest in not suffering but this can be overridden to promote the greater good of humans who are autonomous agents (common view held by many contemporary moral and political philosophers)
   (b) Even if moral orthodox is accepted there are few uses of animals which are necessary (Francione).

3. Challenges to the moral orthodoxy.
   (a) Animals have rights
      (i) based on animals having inherent value (Regan).
      (ii) based on sentiency (Rollin, Ryder).
   (b) Utilitarianism (Singer).
   (c) Contractarianism (Rowlands).

No mainstream political theorist is, or has been, prepared to accept that animals should be regarded as morally equivalent to humans or even morally close to humans. The two main figures in modern political thought that came closest to dispensing with an anthropocentric (or human-centred) ethic were Bentham (1948: 311) and, to a lesser extent, J. S. Mill (1969: 184–7). Bentham's famous statement on animals, written in the *Introduction to the Principles of Morals and Legislation*, originally published in 1789, is worth quoting at length. 'The French have already discovered', he wrote:

> that the blackness of the skin is no reason why a human being should be abandoned without redress to the caprice of a tormentor. It may come one day to be recognized, that the number of the legs, the villosity of the skin, or the termination of the *os sacrum*, are reasons equally insufficient for abandoning a sensitive being to the same fate? What else is it that should trace the insuperable line? Is it the faculty of reason, or, perhaps, the faculty of discourse? But a full-grown horse or dog, is beyond comparison a more rational, as well as a more conversable animals, than an infant of a day, or a week, or even a month old. But suppose the case were otherwise, what would it avail? The question is not, Can they reason? Nor, Can they talk? But, Can they suffer?

Mill, likewise, confirms the applicability of utilitarianism to animals when he wrote, in 1874, that:

> Granted that any practice causes more pain to animals than it gives pleasure to man; is that practice moral or immoral? And if, exactly in proportion as human beings raise their heads out of the slough of selfishness, they do not with one voice answer 'immoral', let the morality of the principle of utility be for ever condemned.

Both Bentham and Mill recognized, then, that a political theory prioritizing sentiency – or the capacity to experience pain and pleasure – would have to include animals as recipients of a considerable moral status, but neither were prepared (unlike a later utilitarian, Peter Singer) to draw the moral egalitarianism that the logic of their position arguably merited. In a letter to the *Morning Chronicle* in 1825, for instance, Bentham wrote that:

> I never have seen, nor ever can see, any objection to the putting of dogs and other inferior animals to pain, in the way of med-ical experiment, when the experiment has a determinate object, beneficial to mankind, accompanied with a fair prospect of the accomplishment of it. But I have a decided and insuperable objection to the putting of them to pain without any such view.
> (quoted in Clarke and Linzey, 1990: 136)

Denying animals equivalent moral significance to humans, of course, is very different from denying them any moral standing whatsoever. Some philosophers, most notably Hobbes (1992: 97), Locke (1988: 271), Kant (1965: 345–6) and Descartes (1912: 43–6), among the key figures in West-ern thought have, adopted this latter position. In these types of accounts, the treatment of animals may raise ethical issues, but animal interests do not matter in their own right. In other words, ill-treating an animal does not infringe any morally important animal interest directly, but we may infringe the interests of other humans in the process. In this case, the obligation to treat an animal well is an indir-ect obligation, since it derives from the direct obligation to another human. Similarly, Locke, Kant and others rule out cruelty to animals on the grounds that those who engage in such behaviour are likely to be inclined to treat humans in the same way.

Descartes' view, that animals were automata, was particu-larly influential. He derived this conclusion from an assertion that animals have no souls, and since soul is necessary for consciousness, he claimed, animals must not be sentient. The popularity of Descartes' theory illustrates how ideologies can serve common practices, in this case justifying what we would now regard as the most barbaric practices on animals at a time before anaesthetic had been developed. As an early anonymous critic of Descartes wrote:

> The scientists administered beatings to dogs with perfect indif-ference and made fun of those who pitied the creatures as if they felt pain. They said the animals were clocks; that the cries

they emitted when struck were only the sound of a little spring that had been touched, but that the whole body was without feeling. They nailed the poor animals up on boards by their four paws to vivisect them to see the circulation of the blood which was a great subject of controversy. (quoted in Regan, 1984: 5)

It is difficult to find many contemporary philosophers who would want to deny that animals are sentient, have interests and as a consequence have moral standing. Behavioural, physiological and evolutionary evidence is put forward to suggest that animals can experience pain (see DeGrazia, 2002: 41–5; Regan, 1984: ch. 1; Rowlands, 2002: 5–9; Singer, 1990: 10–15). Thus, animals act as though they are experiencing pain, and humans and animals have similar physiological reactions to painful stimuli, in the form for instance of the production of endogenous opiates, sweating, increased respiration rate, and the secretion of adrenal hormones. Moreover, awareness of pain is functional for survival since animals can take steps to avoid it. It makes evolutionary sense, therefore, to impute sentiency to human and non-human animals, whereas it does not for plants which do not have the capacity to escape from harm.

One exception to the consensus view that animals are sentient is Carruthers (1992), who doubts the ability of animals to suffer. He provides a contemporary version of the Cartesian theory suggesting that beings that cannot use language cannot think about their experiences or be conscious of them. As a consequence, Carruthers argues, animals cannot feel pain. The vast majority of moral philosophers, however, would agree with DeGrazia (1996: 40, 44) who concludes that: 'Since ethics concerns interests, which animals have, it would seem prima facie, that the treatment of animals is part of the subject matter of ethics' and that the beliefs of those who deny animals have moral standing do not 'require special explanation any more than the existence of white supremacists does'.

The position that nonhuman animals have moral standing has tended to be predicated, then, on the benchmark of sentiency. Whether sentiency is a necessary, as well as a sufficient, characteristic for moral standing is an issue to which we shall return in chapter 6, in the context of attempts to accord moral worth to non-sentient parts of nature. For now, it should be noted that most pro-animal philosophers accord with the view that for an entity to have morally relevant interests it must be sentient. As DeGrazia (1996: 227) comments, 'nonsentient animals, by definition, cannot feel anything, so they cannot have aversive states. Nor can they have any other experience. Nothing matters to them; they care about nothing. They have no concerns or desires.' If this view holds, of course, we can accord no moral standing to non-sentient and non-animal parts of nature. As Singer (1981: 123) explains: 'There is a genuine difficulty in understanding how chopping down a tree can matter *to the tree* if the tree can feel nothing.'

There are some philosophers who want to deny that even sentiency is an adequate grounding for the possession of interests. For example, Kant, and, more recently, Narveson (1987), among others, want to hold that only moral agents – those capable of recognising right from wrong – can be directly morally wronged. As we shall see in chapter 3, Rawls (1972) wants to exclude animals from his theory of justice on similar grounds. Significantly, he does not think, unlike Kant and Narveson, that because of this we only have indirect duties to animals, although the effect of excluding animals from his theory of justice may, as we shall see, amount to the same thing. Frey (1980), similarly, wants to deny that sentiency is an adequate grounding for the possession of interests. Animals, he argues, do not have interests in the sense of being interested in something, as opposed to something being in their interests. In this latter, weaker sense, the concept of interests can be applied to inanimate objects. The former corresponds to having desires which, for Frey, presupposes beliefs which, in turn, animals cannot possess because of their inability to use a language.

To deny that animals have moral significance on a par with humans because they are not moral agents or because they lack a language capacity is one thing, to be discussed further below. To deny them *any* moral worth on these grounds, however, is surely to illegitimately undervalue the importance of sentiency. Whilst the inability of animals to be moral agents may be important at some level, and whilst the use of language undoubtedly enriches existence, it is surely churlish to deny that animals have an interest in not suffering pain whether or not they believe, and can express, that a certain action will lead to the experience of pain. Since animals (as Frey himself accepts) are sentient, then clearly not all interests which do not require beliefs apply to inanimate objects. In reality, too, there is a strong case for saying that many animals do have beliefs, and can act upon them in intelligible ways.

The moral orthodoxy and the exclusion of animals from a community of equals

Accepting that animals have moral standing, of course, does not commit us to moral egalitarianism, and it still remains the case that the vast majority of moral and political philosophers want to deny that animals are anything close to being our moral equals. As was pointed out in the intro-duction to this book, the conventional moral position, in the West at least, governing our relationship with animals – the animal welfare position or the moral orthodoxy as it might be called (see Garner, 1993) – is that while animals have moral standing, in the sense that what we do to them matters to them directly, their moral status is inferior to that of humans. As a result, the moral orthodoxy tells us, humans are entitled to sacrifice the interests of animals if by so doing some significant benefit to the former occurs. Any suffering inflicted, therefore, must be 'necessary' if it is to be morally legitimate. 'Necessity', of course, is a subject-ive term and a judgment as to what constitutes a significant human benefit justifying the infliction of suffering can change radically over time.

Nozick (1974: 39) usefully describes a version of the moral orthodoxy as 'utilitarianism for animals Kantianism for people' in the sense that: 'Human beings may not be used or sacrificed for the benefit of others' whereas 'animals may be used or sacrificed for the benefit of other people or animals *only if* those benefits are greater than the loss inflicted'. This is only one version of the moral orthodoxy in the sense that it is possible to envisage in addition an exclusively utilitarian version whereby both animal *and* human interests could be sacrificed in order to maximize satisfactions or preferences. To remain a version of the moral orthodoxy, of course, utilitarian calculations would have to be weighted in favour of human interests. Bentham must have had something like this in mind, since, as well as being a utilitarian, he also, as we suggested above, regarded animals as morally inferior to humans.

Bentham's problem, as hinted at earlier in this chapter and explored in greater detail in chapter 2, is the difficulty of justifying moral inequality between humans and animals from a utilitarian perspective. As we saw earlier, Bentham himself points out in a famous passage, that 'the question' of moral status is not 'Can they reason? nor, Can they talk? but, Can they suffer?' (1948: 311). In other words, if moral status is based upon sentiency, rather than rationality or language ability, it is difficult to maintain a position of moral inequality between humans and animals. It took more than a century after Bentham was writing for another utilitarian, Peter Singer, to recognize this discrepancy.

The case for the moral orthodoxy depends upon identifying morally relevant differences between humans and animals that allow us to treat them differently. Factual differences, by themselves, are not relevant here, without any additional *argument* that explains why they are morally significant. So, for example, to say simply that species membership alone is sufficient for the attachment of particular kinds of moral worth is to beg the question of what it is about members of the human species that sets it apart morally from other, nonhuman, animals.

One difference, cited, as we saw earlier, by Descartes, and also by Nozick (1974: 48) and Walzer (1983: xii), is that, unlike humans, animals do not have immortal souls and, as a result, have less moral significance than humans. We can dispense with this pretty quickly. First there is the obvious difficulty of proving that souls exist, and if they are thought to exist for humans why not for animals? Some cultures, it might be noted, do extend the existence of a soul beyond the human species. Secondly, it is not clear why possession of a soul is morally significant. Indeed, if anything, it should lead us to the conclusion that we owe obligations to treat animals well since, unlike humans, they do not have the prospect of an afterlife.

The most common method of distinguishing morally between humans and nonhumans is to point to the greater

mental complexity exhibited by the former. A useful starting point is provided by Pluhar (1995: 1–10), who identifies
six categories of beings, not – initially at least – to be confused with actual species types, to whom we might want to
consider attaching degrees of moral standing. First are 'fully-
fledged persons'. This includes 'the highly autonomous and
linguistically sophisticated, who are capable of moral agency
and able to act on principle'. This group is followed by
'persons lower on the autonomy scale', 'self-conscious beings
who have little or no autonomy', 'merely conscious beings',
'living beings with no capacity for consciousness' and
'natural objects or systems'. As indicated at the beginning
of the paragraph, the moral orthodoxy holds that humans
are morally more important than nonhumans because they
are the only species that exhibit 'full-personhood', a category incorporating a variety of skills including rationality,
creativity, intelligence, language use, and autonomy.

To simply list those characteristics that humans possess,
and animals do not – a common tactic of those philosophers who oppose greater moral equality between humans
and animals – is, by itself, insufficient without an accom-
panying explanation as to *why* these particular characteristics are morally significant. A number of different reasons
for the moral superiority of humans over animals have
been derived from the identification of factual differences
relating to human capabilities. A common approach is to
suggest that because animals cannot be moral agents, and
are therefore unable to appreciate what a moral obligation
is, they cannot have the same degree of moral status
accorded to those who are able to recognize and respect the
interests of others, as well as claiming their own rights
(McCloskey, 1979; Ackerman, 1980: 71).

It is largely for this reason that many contemporary
liberal political theorists argue that it is not appropriate to
include animals within a theory of justice. Brian Barry (1999:
95), for instance, comments that 'it does not seem to
me that the concept of justice can be deployed intelligibly
outside the context of relations between human beings',[1]
since only moral agents can be included within a theory of
justice (1989: 7, 10, 272). David Miller (1976: 18), to name
another important scholar, suggests similarly that justice
can only 'involve sentient beings, and paradigmatically it

involves beings who are both sentient and rational'. As Dobson (1998: 66) states: 'Most theories of justice ... simply assume that the list of potential recipients (of justice) is exhausted once contemporary human beings have been taken into account.' More to the point, excluding animals from theories of justice is not a neutral act but reflects an assumption about the inferior moral status of animals. It is this that Dobson is referring to when he remarks that 'any theory of justice which did incorporate animals would be regarded as a second division theory' (1998: 174).

Because of its pre-eminent position within the discipline, it is the exclusion of animals from Rawls' theory of justice which has attracted most attention. Rawls has little to say about animals in *A Theory of Justice*. He writes (Rawls, 1972: 504) that, at least until arguments to the contrary can be devised, human 'conduct toward animals is not regulated by' the principles of justice, because only 'moral persons' are 'entitled to equal justice'. This moral personhood is distinguished by two features. Firstly, moral persons 'are capable of having ... a conception of their good (as expressed by a rational plan of life); and second they are capable of having ... a sense of justice, a normally effective desire to apply and to act upon the principles of justice, at least to a certain minimum degree' (1972: 505). So, only those who can understand what it is to be just, and those who are able to claim it for themselves and respect the rights of others, are entitled to be beneficiaries of justice.

As a result, animals cannot be party to the deliberations of the participants in the original position, and therefore cannot benefit from any of the decisions taken there, since 'the duty of justice is owed to those who could participate in the contractual situation of the original position and act on it' (Rawls, 1963: 301). In other words, whatever else can be hidden behind the veil of ignorance, species membership is not one of them. Richards (1971: 182) makes pretty much the same claim arguing that animals 'lack the capacities of choice and control' that would 'entitle' them to be members of the original position.

Focusing on moral agency is a secondary derivative of a more general set of arguments relating to the full-personhood characteristics said to be possessed by humans. Perhaps the most compelling argument here is that autonomous humans are accorded a higher moral status because their interests can be harmed much more seriously than animals (see Townsend, 1976). Being left free to pursue their life plans is absolutely crucial for the well-being of autonomous humans, but not so crucial for animals, it is alleged, because they have much more limited goals. To take an extreme example, the death of a human is a serious matter, whereas, if we regard animals as merely sentient, then, providing it occurs painlessly, the death of an animal does not raise any moral issues at all. Even if we accept that animals have some mental capacities, the interests of humans – or at least the most significant ones – according to this view, will always prevail because the human level of complexity is always greater. As a result, not only is it a greater wrong to kill a human rather than an animal but it is also a greater wrong, all things being equal, to confine a human against her will.

Animals and full-personhood

From the above it should now be clear that modern liberal political theory has largely accepted the moral orthodoxy, that animals count morally for something but not as much as humans, whose interests take precedence. Because of this, important contemporary liberal political theorists have excluded animals from a theory of justice. While liberal political theorists are sometimes unclear and confused about how to incorporate the recognition that animals have some moral status, there is absolutely no doubt that they are not prepared to grant animals a moral status on a par with humans. Despite this, it is significant that the best known attempts to challenge the moral orthodoxy have come from within the liberal tradition, and these will now be examined.

Exponents of a higher moral status for animals have made two major responses to the argument that it is the capacity of 'full-personhood' that distinguishes humans from animals morally. The first is to reject the view that only humans have full-personhood, the second is to deny that full-personhood has the force claimed for it. This second response can be further divided into at least two separate arguments. The first focuses on the value of sentiency as the benchmark for significant moral standing, and the second seeks to demonstrate the implications of the fact that not all humans have full-personhood.

The first of the responses is probably the weakest one, not least because it is extremely difficult to establish what the mental capacities of animals are. There is now a bewildering range of literature seeking to examine the mental capacities of different species (see reviews in DeGrazia, 1996: chapters 4–7; Pluhar, 1995: 46–55; Regan, 1984: chapters 1 and 2; Regan and Singer, 1989: Part Two; and Rodd, 1990: 79–86. See also Griffin, 1992). It is quite clear that a significant number of nonhuman species exhibit mental capacities that are surprisingly complex and sophisticated. As Pluhar's review of the evidence confirms (1995: 46):

> Many sentient nonhumans apparently have the ability to learn from past experience, to anticipate future events, to change their behaviour in the face of changing circumstances, to carry out short-term plans, and to solve problems in a creative fashion.

As Pluhar continues (57), then, 'no characteristic has yet been found that is *wholly* lacking in nonhumans and wholly present in humans'.

Establishing that, at least some, animals have considerable mental capacities plays a crucial role in one of the most coherent and rigorous critiques of the moral orthodoxy. Tom Regan (1984) seeks to show that at least some animals are, what he calls, 'subjects-of-a-life', possessing enough mental complexity to be morally considerable. Thus, because these animals are self-conscious, have a memory, are capable of having an emotional life and act so as to fulfil their beliefs and preferences, Regan argues that they have a welfare which is capable of being harmed by not only inflictions of pain and deprivation, but also death since it forecloses all possibilities of finding satisfaction in life.

There are a number of problems, however, with an approach that seeks to deny that animals lack full-personhood, or are close enough to it to be morally considerable. Identifying mental complexity as the primary characteristic determining degrees of moral status leads us to two consequences that most animal advocates would be unwilling to endorse. The first is that we will be forced to distinguish morally between different species of nonhumans, and accept that there might be a case for treating them differently. This is the basis, for instance, of the so-called Great Ape Project (Cavalieri and Singer, 1993), a worldwide campaign that seeks to argue the case for the attachment of legal rights to creatures closest to us. Similarly, Steven Wise, a leading American legal scholar, seeks to base his case for the legal rights of animals primarily on apes, arguing that: 'Whatever legal rights these apes may be entitled to spring from the complexities of their minds' (Wise, 2000: 237). Finally, Regan, too, precisely because he uses mental complexity as a criterion for moral worth, is then committed to attaching subject-of-a-life status, and therefore rights, only to mammals aged over one year.

It is undoubtedly politically astute to seek greater legal protection for apes, or even mammals in general, as a species closer to us than other nonhumans, since it may have the effect of putting animal rights on a more secure footing as far as acceptance by decision-makers is concerned. Moreover, by recognizing the moral and therefore legal importance of apes we are making the crucial claim that according considerable moral worth does not stop at the boundary of the human species. As was pointed out above, however, a consequence of this approach is that some nonhuman species are to be regarded as more important morally than others, and are therefore to be treated differently (see Wissenburg, 1998: 178). The danger of such an approach from the perspective of exponents of a higher moral status for animals is that once one accepts the link between mental complexity and moral status, it all but ends the prospects of according moral considerability to those animals that fall on the wrong side of the personhood line.

As a corollary of the above, if the full-personhood criterion is applied rigorously, then it is plausible to exclude all nonhuman animals. In other words, adopting mental complexity as the primary determinant of moral status inexorably leads us to the conclusion that, as Pluhar (1995: 57) correctly recognizes, although animals 'may have lesser degrees of the relevant characteristics ... as far as we know, none can match the capacities of the mature, normal human being. In short, only humans appear to be fully-fledged persons.'

It is clear then that if we accept animals have some degree of mental complexity – as we surely must – their lives become important since, in DeGrazia's words (1996: 232), 'animals ... can be deprived of future satisfactions, goods, or conscious life'. Since, however, it is accepted that humans have greater capacities and, by implication, their lives are worth more (237–40), if we had to choose between saving a human life and an animal life, we are morally entitled, if not compelled, to choose the human. This clearly has important practical ramifications. Using animals in scientific procedures to develop new drug products and test their toxicity, for instance, becomes legitimate if we accept that humans have greater mental complexity and therefore more to lose from death or the loss of some quality of life. The choice to use an animal rather than a human in such procedures is dependent, of course, on the additional assumption that the human in question has the characteristics of full-personhood. This leads to a third problem with seeking to distinguish morally between humans and animals on the grounds of mental complexity, namely that it will controversially exclude from moral considerability those humans – such as the mentally deficient and even young children – who do not have the mental capacities of 'normal' adult humans (see below for more on this point).

The poverty of full-personhood

The second major response to the autonomy claim is to deny its force. There are at least two separate strands to this approach. The first is to accept that animals lack the level of autonomy or 'personhood' possessed by most humans, but to deny that this produces the degree of moral inferiority the moral orthodoxy requires for animals. Nozick, for one, while being a philosopher generally supportive of the moral orthodoxy, has his doubts about connections between mental complexity and moral status (1974: 48). He identifies a typical list of 'important individuating characteristics connected with moral constraints' including 'sentient and self-conscious . . . ; possessing free will; being a moral agent capable of guiding its behaviour by moral principles and capable of engaging in mutual limitation of conduct; having a soul', but then concludes that: 'Leaving aside the last on the list, each of them seems insufficient to forge the requisite connection' with moral status in general and, in particular, the degree to which constraints can be imposed on others to protect those which such characteristics. Later, Nozick does seem to settle on the importance of 'a being able to formulate long-term plans for its life' and, more generally, the pursuit of meaningful life as characteristics worthy of moral status, the possessors of which are candidates for inclusion in a theory of justice. Even then, Nozick adds riders such as why shouldn't we 'interfere with someone else's shaping of his own life', and 'why shouldn't my life be meaningless' (49–50).

If the relationship between full-personhood and an elevated moral status is unclear, then there is an added fillip to the development of a case for according a high moral status for animals on the basis of their sentiency alone. The first consequence of this sentiency view would seem to be that, as the moral orthodoxy claims, the death of animals, providing it is painless, ceases to be of moral significance, whereas the death of humans is clearly of greater importance. If we assume that this is correct, then inflicting suffering on animals only becomes morally legitimate when it can save human lives.

Applying the sentiency view to the main ways in which animals are exploited reveals some interesting results. The conflict, between a human's interest in living and an animal's interest in avoiding pain and suffering, does not necessarily, I think, emerge in the case of animal agriculture, but would depend upon the methods used. Most humans do not need to eat animals to survive and, even if they did, humane methods of killing animals exist. Inflicting suffering in the course of producing animals for food, therefore does remain illegitimate, and this would rule out most modern forms of factory farming which in a variety of ways cause animals to suffer (A. Johnson, 1991; Mason and Singer, 1990). Free-range farming in which animals lead good lives and have painless deaths is not such a moral problem from the perspective of the sentiency view.

In the case of animal experimentation, similar calculations apply. Insofar as research using animals can be shown to
contribute to the longevity of human life then, from the
perspective of the sentiency view, it is morally legitimate.
Much depends, of course, upon the empirical validity of the
claims made by researchers, not an easy thing to evaluate (see
Garner, 1993: ch. 5). In this context, it is no surprise that anti-
vivisectionists have tended to focus, not so much on the
ethical validity of animal research, but on its utility (see,
for instance, Ryder, 1975; Sharpe, 1988). The research on
animals that has no prospect of contributing to the saving
of human life, on the other hand, remains illegitimate. One
might want to say, for instance, that the testing of cosmetic
products on animals for one company, where another has
already tested the same product, is morally suspect.

The sentiency view, while not offering as much as a successful attempt to demonstrate that the mental complexity
of animals is morally significant, clearly offers more than
the moral orthodoxy. This is because the latter allows for the
sacrifice of animal interests in order to promote a range of
human interests, whereas the sentiency view allows it only
if it contributes to the longevity of human life. In particular,
this prohibits animal exploitation on purely economic
grounds, which, given that the economic motive accounts
for a great deal of animal exploitation (see Garner, 1998:
ch. 2), is a significant advance on the moral orthodoxy.

The argument from marginal cases

The second strand of the argument denying the moral significance of full-personhood focuses on the implications of
the fact that some, so-called 'marginal', humans are lacking
in the degree of personhood possessed by normal adult humans. This 'argument from marginal cases' (AMC) accepts
that while only humans can be full persons, not all humans
can be. As a result, those who adopt the full-personhood
criteria for moral status have difficulty explaining why the
moral status of marginal humans, such as small children
and the severely mentally disabled, should not be equivalent to that of normal, adult, nonhuman mammals. Any

attempt to distinguish morally between marginal humans and at least some animals, therefore, becomes illegitimate. If we accept the AMC, it becomes inconsistent, to take one example, for Rawls (1972: 510) to see no problem with including marginal humans as beneficiaries of the decisions taken in the original position and, at the same time, exclude animals. To do so is to adopt a speciesist attitude, illegitimately distinguishing between humans and animals on the grounds of species alone rather than any morally relevant characteristic.

There is some evidence that Rawls, for one, was aware of the problem here. Johnson (1976: 128–9) notes that in *A Theory of Justice* Rawls makes a subtle change to his earlier position. In an earlier article, *A Sense of Justice*, he (1963: 284) argues that 'it is necessary and sufficient that he be capable, to a certain minimum degree, of a sense of justice' in order to qualify for membership in the original position. By the time of *A Theory of Justice* (1972: 505; 512) however, the capacity for moral personality' is now only a 'sufficient condition for being entitled to equal justice', and 'I have not maintained that the capacity for a sense of justice is necessary in order to be owed the duties of justice'. This latter position, of course, raises the possibility that those not possessing moral personhood, including animals, are still entitled to be beneficiaries of the deliberations in the original position. Rawls, though, does not follow though the logic of his argument since he still wants to maintain (1972: 512; 504; 505) that 'it does seem that we are not required to give strict justice anyway to creatures lacking this capacity', and again that 'Our conduct towards animals is not regulated by these principles, or so it is generally believed', and finally that animals are 'presumably' excluded from equal basic rights.

This apparent logical flaw in Rawls' account is difficult to explain. However, it is indicative of the problems associated with trying to discriminate between humans and animals on the grounds of mental capabilities since it appears likely that Rawls is uncomfortable with the recognition that, by insisting upon moral personhood as the primary qualification for justice, he then excludes those humans without the entry qualification, thereby leaving himself open to the criticism employed in the AMC. At one point in *A Theory of Justice*, Rawls (1972: 248–9) does seem to recognize the force of the argument when he writes that the participants in the original position

> will want to insure themselves against the possibility that their powers are undeveloped and they cannot rationally advance their interests, as in the case of children; or that through some misfortune or accident they are unable to make decisions for their good, as in the case of those seriously injured or mentally disturbed.

For the most part, though, he dismisses the challenge that marginal humans make to his theory.

Rawls's confusion about animals then stems from a conflict within his thought. On the one hand, he recognizes that if one includes those humans who do not meet the moral personhood criterion, then there is nothing to prevent the inclusion of animals. On the other hand, he brings with him a predetermined assumption that animals should not be included within a theory of justice, which he is intent upon maintaining. This would help to explain the unconvincing prevarication – 'so it is generally believed', 'it does seem', 'presumably' – which litters Rawls' account of the moral status of animals.

If we accept the AMC, two options present themselves. We can conclude, in the 'categorical' version, that *because* marginal humans have rights, or maximum moral significance, then so do at least some animals. Alternatively, in the 'biconditional' version, we can conclude that *if* marginal humans have rights or are regarded as having maximum moral significance, then so do at least some animals (Pluhar, 1995: 63–4). This latter version, of course, is weaker because it could be used to justify excluding both animals and marginal humans from full-personhood.

Holding the biconditional view, then, commits us to accepting that if we are prepared to exploit animals in order to benefit those humans who have full-personhood, it is inconsistent not to consider using marginal humans in a similar way. In other words, if we are prepared to inflict suffering on animals, to experiment on them and eat them and so forth, we should be prepared to treat marginal humans in the same way. The logic of this argument has been recognised, most notably, by Frey (1987; 2002). Whilst he is right to say that the medical profession has to make

decisions about who would benefit most from the utilisa-
tion of scarce resources, and this can involve considerations of levels of personhood, Frey is committing himself
to more than, say, allowing a seriously defective human
being to die rather than administering expensive medical
treatment. Indeed, he has to sanction inflicting pain on an
animal in a laboratory experiment. The fact that this would
not be in accord with our moral intuition would appear to
illustrate not only that the rationality criterion is morally
flawed but also that it is morally wrong to exploit animals
for food or medical research or whatever.

There have been a number of responses to the AMC. The
most obvious response has been that infants and children
should not be regarded as 'marginal' because they have the
potential for rationality (Rawls, 1963: 303; 1972: 509). However, while this is true for the bulk of children, it should be
noted that this rather misses the point of the argument.
Full-personhood is recognized as a key determinant of differential treatment because at any one point in time those
with the constituent characteristics can be harmed in much
more damaging ways than those without, and there is no
dispute that small children do not possess these characteristics to the same degree as normal adult humans. Therefore,
potentiality is logically different from actuality, and without
an argument explaining why potential persons are the same
as actual persons, it does not seem possible to include the
former as full-persons, and does not explain why, if we are
prepared to exploit animals, why we should not be morally
entitled to exploit infants with a similar degree of personhood (Pluhar, 1995: 107–10).

Whatever the case for children, this still leaves the issue
of adults who have severe mental incapacities, those, in
other words, who have no potential for autonomy or moral
personhood. A well-rehearsed debate on the validity of the
argument from marginal cases exists (Pluhar, 1995). The
case against is based, in addition to the arguments above,
on such claims that it is the characteristics of the normal
members of a species that should be morally significant;
that kinship is a key characteristic (Holland, 1984; Midgley,
1983); that the capabilities of even marginal humans is
underestimated; that humans have a self-interest in protecting marginal humans since any of us 'normal' humans

might become marginal in the future or that we will have relatives who will want us to be treated with respect (Carruthers, 1992: 115–16).

Focusing on our self-interested desire to be subject to respect should we become 'marginal' humans at some point in the future would appear to be a powerful argument for treating such humans with dignity now, and is therefore a forceful challenge to the argument from marginal cases. Of course, we might want to argue that self-interest does not exhaust all of our moral sensibilities, and that consistency, for instance, might be equally valid. More pertinently, as an answer to this and other criticisms above, is the crucial distinction, identified by Pluhar (1995: 63–4), between the 'bioconditional' and 'categorical' versions of the argument from marginal cases (see above). Only if we hold the former version do questions about the dignity of marginal humans arise. Acceptance of the latter version, which animal advocates must support, necessitates treating *both* marginal humans and animals with respect.

Despite these attempts at challenging its validity, the argument from marginal cases represents a powerful challenge to the assumption that full-personhood should be the key benchmark for moral considerability. If it is correct, demonstrating equivalence in moral significance between humans and animals requires only that we show that the mental capacities of animals are at least as great as those of marginal humans, coupled with a rejection of the view that we should treat marginal humans and animals differently from normal humans. If this is successful, there is nothing stopping us from accepting that the moral orthodoxy is flawed. Similarly, if liberal philosophers such as Rawls persist with the rationality criterion for justice, they can certainly exclude animals but only at the cost of also denying coverage possibly to children and, with greater certainty, to mentally deficient adults.

The contractarian approach

The attempts, of which there are many, to utilize the contractarian approach to the advantage of animals have primarily consisted of the devising of amendments to Rawls' original position and veil of ignorance. As we shall see later on in the chapter, the contractarian approach, duly amended to include the interests of animals, is regarded by its major exponent as a preferable alternative to the rights and utilitarian models of expressing the elevated moral status for animals (Rowlands, 1998). It is also the case that this approach stands alone as an alternative means of justifying an elevated moral status for animals. Thus, the argument goes, there is no need to engage in the debates about the importance of full-personhood, sentiency and the argument from marginal cases. Rather, all we have to do is to establish that animals can be the beneficiaries of decisions taken by participants in the original position, and this guarantees, in effect, a moral equivalence between humans and animals. This section will try to demonstrate that the case for excluding animals from being beneficiaries of Rawls' theory of justice is weak. It will be argued later in the chapter, however, that this does not mean that the contractarian approach is, by itself, the most effective means of establishing a higher moral status for animals.

The most sustained attempt to promote a contractarian approach to animal ethics is provided by Rowlands (1998). He argues that the protection of animal interests can be incorporated into contractarian theories, in that just as specific human abilities, and more general characteristics such as age, gender, race and class are hidden behind the veil of ignorance, rationality is an equally undeserved natural advantage which also ought to be hidden. By enlarging the uncertainty in the original position, or 'thickening the veil' as Wenz (1988: 249) puts it, the contracting parties would have to take into account the possibility that they might lack rationality, or moral personhood, which leaves open the possibility that they could turn out to be either 'defective' humans or, as a logical extension, animals. Therefore, the identity of species is added to those things excluded behind the veil of knowledge, and given Rawls' assumptions about the risk-minimising strategy the participants in the original position would adopt (the so-called maximin strategy), they would have to take into account the possibility that they might end up as members of another species.

A failure to include species, it is argued, would be tantamount to speciesism in the same way that to allow knowledge of race or gender in the original position would be racist and sexist (Vandeveer, 1979: 374). Rawls' 'difference principle', or at least part of it, that social and economic inequalities are to be arranged so that they are to the greatest benefit of the least advantaged, would now benefit all those sentient beings, including animals and the most vulnerable humans, as the least able to defend their interests. In practice, this 'would entail that many widespread, standard ways that animals are treated are grossly unjust' (Vandeveer, 1979: 373).

A number of criticisms have been made of the attempt to adapt Rawls. A familiar retort is that rationality, and in particular a sense of morality, is an essential criterion for the contracting parties since how else can they deliberate in the original position, and how else can they keep to the agreement made? (Pritchard and Robinson, 1981: 60–1). The first response to this might be to challenge the view that animals do not have a sense of justice. Some animals, like some humans, for instance, pair for life, are faithful spouses and parents, and show loyalty and courage (Elliot, 1984: 96–7).

A more promising response is to argue that, as in the context of the AMC, it is possible to challenge the view that all humans are always imbued with a capacity to understand what it is to be just. But, if we include those humans as beneficiaries of decisions taken by the participants in the original position, there is a compelling argument for including animals too. To achieve this goal all Rawls has to do is to change the terms of his social contract so that it is not what individuals are like in the original position that matters but what they eventually turn out like. As Rowlands (1998: 123) points out: 'The fact that the *framers* of the contract must be conceived of as rational agents does not entail that the *recipients* of the protection afforded by the contract must be rational agents.' If that was the case then Rawls would have difficulty incorporating children and mental defectives as recipients, yet, as we saw earlier, he clearly wants to do so (Rawls, 1972: 509–10). As Brian Barry (1989: 204) points out:

> There is no reason in principle why we could not derive protec-
> tion for the interests of nonhuman animals by using the
> machinery of the original position. All we have to do is to
> extend its scope to include representatives of all sentient
> beings.

This done, Barry (1989: 212) is right to conclude that 'if a
day-old infant can be represented in the original position,
why not a monkey or a dog?'

Another criticism of the attempt to incorporate animals
as beneficiaries of the deliberations in the original position
is that by demoting rationality in the way Rowlands and
others suggests is to open the door to the inclusion of the
whole of the natural world as recipients of justice (Wissenburg, 1999). Ecocentric Greens would want to go this far
(see Thero, 1995: 99–100), but the demotion of rationality
does not necessarily lead us to this outcome, not least because animals can still be distinguished from the rest of
nature by their sentiency and, albeit limited, autonomy (see
chapter 6). Yet another criticism is that the enlargement of
uncertainty 'stretches the imagination too far'. 'We cannot
imagine', Wissenberg (1993: 17) argues, 'what it is like to
be irrational or immoral, or even psychotic; we certainly
cannot think ourselves into the position of an animal'. To
allow the possibility that participants in the original position may turn out to be animals, therefore, 'enormously com-
plicates calculations' (Pritchard and Robinson, 1981: 60).

There are a number of responses to this last criticism. In
the first place, as Brent Singer (1988: 223) points out, 'to
argue that something is difficult – even extremely difficult
– is no argument against it being morally right'. Moreover,
why should it be more difficult to work out the wants and
desires of animals than of humans? Indeed, there may be a
case for saying that 'the primary interests of nonhuman
animals are often more straightforward than the primary
interests of human beings' (Singer, 1988: 223–4). In its
conventional interpretation, Rawls' contractarianism does
require us to empathize with a wide variety of situations.
It is not clear why imagining being an animal is any more
difficult than imagining being a human who is mentally deficient in some way, and yet Rawls, as we have
seen, is unwilling to exclude such humans as recipients of
justice.

Rights, utility and contractarianism

If it is established that animals have a higher moral status than the orthodoxy allows then a second-order question arises. This is to which general theory can we attach the moral status of humans *and* animals? In the animal ethics literature, as in ethics in general, the major division has been between rights and utilitarianism, and, in particular, the advocacy of the former by Regan (1984) and the latter by Singer (1990). A third possible approach from within the liberal tradition is the contractarian case for a higher moral status for animals discussed above. This is a variant of the rights position and claims an objectivity which, it is argued, the other two approaches lack.

The dimensions of the Regan/Singer debate follow conventional lines. The former points to the benefits of focusing on individual sovereignty and condemns utilitarianism for its willingness to sacrifice individuals in pursuit of maximizing the aggregate amount of preference satisfactions. The latter, by contrast, emphasizes the flexibility of utilitarianism against the rigidity of rights and the difficulty of choosing between competing rights claims.

A fundamental problem with rights theory is the difficulty of basing moral principles on natural law and natural rights. In other words, on what grounds do they exist, or are they, as Bentham famously asserted, 'nonsense upon stilts'? (see Waldron, 1987). The obvious way of establishing the validity of rights is in terms of their derivation from God, but this is not, for most now, a valid enough reason. Regan's attempt to base it instead on the concept of inherent value arguably does not get us much further since it is a rather 'mysterious' concept devoid of clear meaning and origins (Rowlands, 1998: 10–12). Rowlands (1998: 115–18) argues that the concept becomes much more coherent if we replace the objective 'inherent value' with the subjective 'inherently valued'. Such a move, of course, while making more sense, has the consequence of depending on individual perceptions of the status of animals, thereby failing to meet Regan's intention of granting inherent value across the board by applying objective criteria. Others who argue for the according of rights to animals focus not so much on the inherent value of animals but on their sentiency (see Ryder,

1989: 325–9 and Rollin, 1981). The problem with this approach, however, is that – if the argument from marginal cases is rejected – then sentiency alone, as we saw, does not provide us with the moral equivalency between humans and animals – and in particular an equal right to life – that most advocates of animal rights argue for.

The concept of abstract rights has been associated, in particular, with the liberal tradition, and has been challenged from a variety of alternative ideological perspectives. Marxists, for instance, focus on the alleged gap between the formal possession of rights and their substantive enjoyment, and this traditional critique has been specifically applied to the case of animals (see chapter 5). Similarly, green political theorists have criticized the concept for its lack of ecological sophistication (see chapter 6). Rights have also been challenged from within the liberal tradition by utilitarians, and Peter Singer (1979, 1990) is noted for his utilitarian approach to animal ethics.

Locating utilitarianism within the liberal pantheon requires some explanation not least because there would seem to be a conflict between the priority utilitarians give to happiness over freedom and a conflict between the utilitarian imperative to maximize utility, whatever the consequences for individual interests, and the liberal emphasis on the protection of individuals against the collective (Rowlands, 1998: 49–54). The first response here is to say that freedom and happiness are not necessarily conflictual objectives. Bentham, for one, thought that individuals were usually the best judges of their own interests and therefore, in his thought, there was a presumption in favour of freedom and non-intervention. The relationship between freedom and happiness, however, remains contingent and utilitarian are bound to limit freedom if happiness is thought to be at stake.

Utilitarianism's emphasis on the aggregation of interests is more difficult to reconcile with liberalism. One response is to say that utilitarianism does, consistently with liberalism, require that each person ought to be treated with, to borrow Singer's language, equal consideration. Both liberalism and utilitarianism, in other words, adopt the same individualistic premises. Thus, Bentham (1948: chap. 1, sec. 4), in line with this, suggests that the community 'is a fictitious body composed of the individual persons who are considered as constituting as it were its members. The interest of the community then is what? – the sum of the interests of the several members who compose it'. Moreover, liberal neutrality and toleration of different value systems is also served by utilitarianism since, as Sandel (1984: 2) points out: 'Maximising utility does not require judging people's values, only aggregating them'. Despite this, the equal consideration of individual interests is not the same as protecting individual rights as a desired outcome and, although there is some dispute about this (see Rowlands, 1998: 72–6), would not appear to rule out the sacrifice of the most fundamental interests of individuals.

It is one of the alleged advantages of Singer's utilitarian approach that it is more flexible than the rights approach. In the first place, it requires a weighing up of the interests affected by any particular action. In addition, it also allows for a greater recognition that the interests of animals and humans differ. So, the equal consideration of interests does not equate with identical treatment since it is concerned with identifying relevantly similar interests. This allows us, for instance, to distinguish between the undoubtedly different levels of harm that can be inflicted on 'normal' and 'defective' humans, and on nonhuman animals.

Singer has come in for some criticism from the animal rights camp for this very flexibility. It is argued, by Regan amongst others, that no particular exploitation of animals is automatically ruled out as illegitimate, because they are contingent upon a utilitarian calculation (Regan, 1984: 200–31. See also Rowlands, 1998: 83–6, 154–7; Pluhar, 1995: 182–4; Wenz, 1988: 165–6). This might mean that the overall benefits of meat eating and animal experimentation – in terms, for instance, of employment and human and animal health, might outweigh the costs. Not only does Singer's utilitarianism allow for the possibility of the sacrifice of the fundamental interests of animals, but also, because utilitarianism is fundamentally concerned about the maximization of pleasures or the satisfaction of wants, it has difficulty with morally condemning painless death, whatever the circumstances. The only definite consideration is to make sure that, in the event of painless killing, adequate replacements are made to ensure the equivalent aggregate level of satisfaction is retained (Singer, 1979). This leaves open the possibility that, for instance, a reformed system of animal agriculture, removing the worst excesses of factory farming, could conceivably meet Singer's demands. Similarly, Singer might also have to regard as morally legitimate scientific procedures, which used anaesthetics, and which practiced euthanasia before their effects wore off.

It is incorrect to conclude from the above, however, that Singer's views are equivalent to those of the moral orthodoxy. There is a crucial difference between the place of humans in Singer's utilitarianism and the moral orthodoxy. The key is that Singer advocates the equal consideration of interests so that it is conceivable that it might be justifiable to sacrifice the interests of humans if, by so doing, the aggregate level of want satisfaction for humans and animals is increased. So, unlike the moral orthodoxy where humans are protected by rights, the killing of humans is not ruled out by Singer's version of utilitarianism. In reality, Singer is asking us to reflect upon our reaction to the possibility of sacrificing significant human interests in order to promote an aggregate good. If we are horrified at the prospect of using humans in painful scientific experiments, Singer would argue, we should condemn with equal vigour the use of animals. As a corollary, of course, if we are prepared to use animals, there is no moral reason why we should not be prepared to use humans.

An apparent advantage of amending Rawls to incorporate animals is that it helps to minimize the oft-heard critique of conventional rights and utilitarian approaches that the discussion of values or norms, and in this case the elevated moral status of animals, is inherently subjective. The advantage of Rawls, it is argued, is that he derives his normative principle of justice from the procedural device of the original position, and therefore, if animals can be successfully included within it, their elevated moral status can be said to derive more or less objectively from the logic of his heuristic device, thereby avoiding contestable notions of the value of sentiency or rationality and so on.

We should not make too much of these claims made for the contractarian approach. Rawls himself accepts that radically different principles might derive from the adoption of a contractarian approach, and therefore we have to test the conclusions against our moral intuitions. The process of weighing up principles derived from the original position against our intuition, making adjustments where we think necessary, Rawls describes as 'reflective equilibrium' (1972: 20). Such a process, it might be argued, makes the contractarian approach redundant – or at least much less significant – since the conclusions deriving from it are dependent on, or at the very least influenced by, pre-existing values. Rawls brings to the social contract, for instance, his ideological 'baggage' that social and economic inequalities are undeserved, and that people will tend to choose freedom ahead of equality, and his original position is arguably designed in such a way that it produces results consistent with his prior value system (Kymlicka, 1990: 66–8; Wenz, 1988: 252). Dworkin (1975) similarly, argues that at the heart of Rawls' contractarianism is a deep commitment to the right of each individual to equal concern and respect.

It is this same primacy that Rawls places on intuition, and predetermined notions of what should be included within a theory of justice, that enables him to exclude animals as beneficiaries. Rather than occurring as a result of deliberations in the original position, therefore, Rawls excludes animals by arguing that only those who are 'moral persons' can be included. This is an artificial and indiscriminate decision that has nothing to do with his heuristic device that some claim was designed to produce a more or less neutral theory of justice. Similarly, though, the inclusion of animals also results from predetermined notions of their moral worth, and the respective value of rationality and sentiency as guides to moral considerability. In other words, in both cases – the denial and assertion of justice for animals – the important normative work is done before the social contract is put into motion. As Wenz (1988: 252) comments, 'when people tinker with the details of the original position in order to obtain certain results, it is their predetermined notions of right and wrong that are responsible for the results'.

Conclusion

This chapter has explored a range of arguments justifying the moral orthodoxy and in support of the granting of a higher moral status for animals. Two main conclusions can be derived from this evidence. In the first place, the arguments employed have almost exclusively been provided from within the liberal tradition. Rights, utilitarian and contractarian approaches; the use of rationality; logical argument; the focus on individualism, have a familiar liberal sound to them. Secondly, the arguments for increasing the moral status of animals, for this author at least, appear to be robust and, in some case, unanswerable. This, however, is only part of the story. As the next two chapters will reveal, there are significant difficulties with defending animal interests from within the liberal tradition, leading to the possibility that it may be necessary to look elsewhere for a more appropriate ideological home for animal protection.

Note

1 Despite this, Barry is more sympathetic to the notion of animal protection than Rawls. As we shall see, he recognizes the case for including animals in the original position. Moreover, in a later work (2001: 40) he remarks revealingly that 'I can see no answer to the moral case for vegetarianism'. Given this, it is something of a puzzle why Barry still insists upon excluding animals from a theory of justice.

2

Liberalism, property and the representation of animals in the legal system

In the previous chapter we saw that the best known critiques of the moral orthodoxy concerning our relationship with nonhuman animals – invoking rights, utilitarian and contractarian arguments – have been developed within the liberal tradition. It might be thought from this that liberalism offers the most appropriate ideological location for the protection of animal interests. However, arguments presented in the following two chapters suggest that it is premature to grant this status to liberalism. This is partly because it is not clear that granting rights to animals is sufficient for their interests to be protected, an argument explored in this chapter and again in chapter 5. Arguably more significantly, certain themes central to liberal thought would seem to be detrimental to animal interests, if the case for a higher moral status is rejected. In other words, there are good reasons for thinking that the moral orthodoxy, which purports to offer animals a modicum of protection, is seriously compromised in liberal societies, and is therefore an ineffective protector of animal interests.

There are three main strands to this argument, two of which are dealt with in this chapter and the third in chapter 3. In the first place, it should be noted that mainstream academic political theory, let alone governments and civil societies in liberal democratic countries, have not come close to accepting and acting upon liberal-derived critiques of the moral orthodoxy. It will be suggested that there are a number of practical reasons for this reluctance to grant a higher moral status to animals, which should lead us to question whether liberal democratic societies will ever accept the consequences of taking this egalitarian step. The second strand is the impact of the property status of animals in liberal societies, which, some scholars have argued, is inimical to even the most basic protection of animal interests. Third, liberalism is further problematic in the sense that if animals are excluded from a theory of justice, as many contemporary liberal political theorists seek to assert, then they become potential victims of the core liberal principle of moral pluralism. It is suggested in chapter 3 that this view, that no society or state should impose a moral code beyond that which ensures the basic protection of individual humans, comes into conflict with, and can undermine, the protection of basic animal interests.

Liberalism and animal rights

It is no accident that the major attempts to develop a critique of the moral orthodoxy have come from within the liberal tradition. There is, firstly, the pragmatic point that a theory of animal protection developed from within this tradition is more likely to be acceptable, given that liberalism is central to Western thought and practice. The work of liberal animal advocates quite consciously uses the language of reason and rationality, much more acceptable to a liberal audience than the vocabulary of compassion, of caring and feeling, which would seem to be appropriate in the discourse of animal suffering and exploitation. It is also the case, secondly, that it is possible to invoke certain liberal values in support of the enhancement of the moral status of animals (Rowlands, 1998: 38–61). First, its *reformist* character allows change and improvement to existing institutions and practices; second, it is a *universalistic* principle and therefore can be used to justify the liberation of animals everywhere; third, its *individualism* allows us to focus on the protection of individual animals; and fourth, its *egalitarianism* can be used to advocate equality across the species barrier.

Despite this, in liberal democratic societies such as Britain the moral orthodoxy, which confirms the moral superiority of humans, predominates over animal rights and, for good reasons, is likely to continue to do so. Significant human interests in such societies, or any kind of society for that matter, are rarely, if ever, sacrificed to uphold the interests of animals. While there is considerable support in some countries for reforms to the way animals are raised for food, for instance, progress in achieving them is painfully slow and the number of vegetarians and vegans remains small. This point can be illustrated by reference to the recent British campaign to ban the live export of farm animals. Benton and Redfearn's study (1996: 51) reveals that the large protest constituency generated was a product of eschewing rights language in preference to a broad welfarist agenda. Thus:

> The limiting of the protests to identifiable 'welfare' targets has been crucial in maintaining the breadth of public support that the campaign continues to enjoy. A large poster draped from a Colchester pub read 'You Don't Have to Stop Eating Meat to Care – Ban Live Exports'.

Consideration of other animal issues reveals a similar pattern. For example, whilst there is considerable support for ending the use of animals in the laboratory for 'trivial' procedures – such as the toxicity testing of cosmetics – fewer are prepared to sanction a prohibition on the use of animals in medical research, where significant benefits to humans are possible, or alleged to be so. Likewise, there tends to be considerable support for banning fox hunting, the use of animals in circuses and the keeping of animals in fur farms, not because animals are regarded as having rights, but because the animal suffering involved in these various practices is regarded as unnecessary, or less necessary than, say, some uses of animals in the laboratory.

It is this non-anthropocentric character of the animal rights movement which holds the key to explaining why it has achieved relatively little progress.[1] Along with the deep ecology movement, animal rights is the only cause that seeks to advance the interests of nonhuman species, *even when* these interests are in conflict with the significant interests of humans. It is not surprising that research by Opotow (1993) found that concern for animals diminishes as the severity of conflict between animals and humans increases. Perhaps more surprising – particularly in the light of claims that support for animal rights is built upon concern for those animals, such as nonhuman primates, who are most like us (Tester, 1991) – was that this survey also found that the usefulness of a species to us provided a more positive indicator of concern than the similarity of the species to us. From this it is easy to see the reason campaigns designed to protect wild animals tend to be more numerous and successful than those involving domesticated animals, since there are considerable human benefits – whether aesthetic, economic or health-based – to be had from protecting them (see chapter 6).

Clearly, then, a movement that is painted as promoting a cause that will, rightly or wrongly, damage some human interests is going to face peculiar problems. As Gray (1997: 162) accurately points out:

> There is little utility for practical men and women in observing that the demands of human well-being may be at odds with those of other animal species. After all, public policy is formed and implemented by human beings. No measure that does not promise a benefit to humans is likely to gain a hearing.

Animals, then, cannot campaign for their own liberation, and it requires an unprecedented level of altruism from members of a species who stand to lose from the protection of animals, to fulfil this objective on behalf of them. As Wise (2000, 13–14) astutely recognizes: 'The problem for nonhuman animals is that they can neither fight nor write. Well, they can fight a little ... But they are uniformly terrible at organized warfare against humans, and we are excellent at slaughtering them'. It should also be pointed out here that the argument from altruism sketched here is, intellectually, an *alternative* to the argument from justice – that animals are deserving of moral considerability because of the reasons explored in this book. Politically, it may be that the protection of animals advocated by the argument from justice will only be possible through the success of the argument from altruism.

It is the moral orthodoxy, then, which tends to hold sway in mainstream public debates about our treatment of animals. However, in theory at least, there is still considerable scope for improving the welfare of animals, even though animal rights are not on the agenda. Where it can be shown that animal suffering is regarded as unnecessary because it serves no useful human purpose, or where the human sacrifices involved are not regarded as substantial, improvements in the way animals are treated become possible. In Britain, as in many other countries, the laws relating to the welfare of farm and laboratory animals fit this pattern. For instance, the statute regulating animal experimentation in Britain specifically requires researchers to balance the pain and distress their work inflicts on animals with the benefits that work is likely to produce (Morton, 1989). Doubts have been raised, however, about the utility of the moral orthodoxy in liberal societies and these will be considered in the rest of this chapter and the next.

The panacea of property

The right to acquire, use and dispose of property as one sees fit is regarded as one of the most important natural rights, and one of the defining characteristics of classical liberalism. It is held by some animal activists and legal scholars that the fact that animals are the property of humans severely compromises the effective protection of their interests. There are two main claims being made here. The first claim is that the notion of the equal consideration of animal and human interests cannot be achieved unless the property status of the former is removed. More contentiously, it is also argued by some that the property status of animals is not even compatible with the most basic protection of animals (see Francione, 1995 and 1996; Kelch, 1998; Wise, 2000). This latter argument, described by Tannenbaum, (1995) as the 'activist's view' of the law relating to animals, contains a number of interrelated claims; first, that animals are regarded as little more than inanimate objects; second, that despite the existence of anti-cruelty statutes the most fundamental interests of animals are more often than not sacrificed in favour of even trivial human interests; and finally, that these statutes are invariably concerned, not with the direct protection of animals, but with the moral character of humans who, without legal constraints, might be tempted to behave in an inhumane fashion.

There is an assumption amongst many animal law scholars, and many in the animal rights movement, that abolishing the legal status of animals as the property of humans will open the door to an animal rights Garden of Eden where liberated animals will cease to be systematically exploited by humans. There is a strong case for agreeing with the proposition that abolishing the property status of animals is a necessary step towards the achievement of an animal rights agenda where, to all intents and purposes, animals are regarded as the moral equals of humans. However, such a move is by no means a sufficient step. That is, there are a number of reasons to suppose that, without any additional changes, animals would continue to be exploited even if their property status was abolished.

One of the reasons for the supposed irrelevance of property rights here centres on a Marxist-inspired critique of rights in general, which focuses on the gap between the legal application of entitlement to rights and the achievement of genuine benefits deriving from them in practice (Lukes, 1985). We shall return to this in chapter 5. More practically, here, it should be noted that even many of those animals not regarded as the property of private citizens have been mercilessly exploited. Wild animals, of course, come into this category. There are various ways in which ownership of wild animals can and has been conferred, but without this confirmation animals in the wild are not owned by private citizens, although, equally, they are not regarded as possessors of rights either. Conversely, it should be noted that there are cases where domestication, and therefore ownership, has had positive implications for wild animals. For instance, although contentious, it might be suggested that those animals, from species with little or no chance of surviving in the wild, that are kept in zoos with very good records of environmental enrichment benefit from human ownership.

In a similar light, private property in land can have positive animal welfare results. One of the strategies of the British League Against Cruel Sports, for instance, is to buy land in hunting areas (Thomas, 1983: 89–91). The League now owns about 2,000 acres of land in 30 separate sites in the west of England. Not only does this prevent some animals from being killed by hunters, it can also lead to extensive publicity whenever a hunt trespasses on the land. On a related theme, the League also provides legal assistance to those whose property – whether companion animals or inanimate objects – has been damaged by hunts. Equally important has been the successful campaign to persuade the National Trust – a private British owner of land and historic buildings – to ban deer-hunting on its land. This decision, confirmed in April 1997, severely restricts most of the deer hunts in the West of England. Finally, it has been known for legislative protection to benefit *only* those animals that are captive. For instance, the British Protection of Animals Act 1911, a general anti-cruelty statute, only provided protection to those animals that were regarded as captive when an offence took place (Sweeney, 1990). This legal loophole was closed in 1996, by the Wild Mammals (Protection) Act.

It is undoubtedly the case that the plight of wild animals tends to get more publicity, and more sympathetic coverage, than domesticated animals, in factory farms and laboratories. It might be thought that this has something to do with the fact that wild animals are seen as free and not the property of humans to exploit as they see fit. Whilst the majestic nature of at least some species of wild animals allowed to roam freely is undoubtedly a factor in courting positive public opinion, it should also be reiterated that the motives for protecting wild animals are primarily anthropocentric ones (see chapter 6). Thus, far from being free from human exploitation, wild animals are used by humans for a variety of purposes – hunting for food, tourism, aesthetic pleasure and so on – despite the fact that they are not regarded as property in the same sense as domesticated animals are.

Animal welfare within the property paradigm

Altering their status as the property of humans would undoubtedly increase the prospects of protecting animals. Clearly, whilst animals remain property they cannot have the full entitlement of rights, and especially the right to be free from exploitation, that advocates of animal rights insist they should have. Ownership implies entitlements to the owner and, while – as we shall see below – it does not necessarily translate into a right to do as one pleases, the case for restricting property rights has to be made on each occasion and for good reason. In other words, whilst animals remain property they cannot be said to have rights in the strict sense of an entitlement, in the negative sense of the term, to be left alone unless an infringement can be justified. The obvious parallel here is human slavery where, irrespective of the fact that the treatment meted out to slaves was not universally negative, they were regarded as lacking some basic entitlement that was granted to free humans.[2] The consequences of abolishing the property status of animals is summed up neatly by Tannenbaum (1995: 179), who writes that:

> It would be impossible to buy or sell animals, to pass their ownership on through inheritance, to tax their value, or to use them in a myriad of ways (such as sources of food and fiber) that will continue to be regarded as acceptable by the great majority of people.

In other words, if the aim is to secure for animals the equal consideration of their interests with those of humans, then it *is* necessary, albeit not necessarily sufficient, to abolish their property status.

Still open to debate, however, is the *degree* to which animals can be protected whilst they still have property status. Logically, this will be dependent upon the degree to which any particular state and society is willing to sanction interfering in an individual's property right in order to benefit animals. In theory, such an eventuality is clearly possible, even to the point where the state can prohibit private citizens from owning animals (Tannenbaum, 1995: 142). Even within rights discourse, rights are not necessarily regarded as absolute since there are always occasions in which we have to consider intervening in order to protect other rights. Many, from other traditions such as utilitarianism, of course, also recognize a case for sacrificing the important interests of individuals in pursuit of the general good or the maximization of preferences. In practice, all societies are prepared to intervene to restrict property rights in order to promote other desired ends (Tannenbaum, 1995: 141–2). This does not just apply to sentient animals. There are even limits to

what individuals may do with inanimate objects they own
– such as buildings regarded as important for historical and/
or aesthetic reasons – if infringing property rights is perceived to result in the securing of other valued human ends.

It is undoubtedly the case that there are many poor
animal welfare laws, that animals often do lose out to
relatively trivial human interests, either because the laws
have limited scope, or because courts interpret them in a
conservative fashion or because they are badly enforced
(see Francione, 1995; Garner, 1998; Kelch, 1998: 540–4;
Wolfson, 1996). It is maintained here though that the existence of poor statutory protection for animals has nothing
to do with the property status of animals, and that those
who link the two are making an assumption that is not
supported by the evidence. It is clearly possible to envisage
a situation where anticruelty regulations 'trump property
rights when they conflict' (Wicklund, 1997: 574) and effective animal protection statutes do just this.

There is a case for saying that the general anti-cruelty
statutes that depend upon the difficult task of proving unnecessary suffering are not particularly effective, although
even these have something to be said for them (Radford,
1999: 703). As Tannenbaum (1995: 172), remarks, 'there is
nothing in cruelty laws that prohibits the legal system from
giving certain animal interests greater weight than has
been done in the past'. It should be noted that the general
anticruelty statute approach is not the only animal welfare
model. In Britain, for instance, the value of the primary statutes governing animal agriculture – the 1968 Agricultural
(Miscellaneous Provisions) Act – and animal experimentation – the 1986 Animals (Scientific Procedures) Act – is not
so much in the basic unnecessary cruelty provisions they
both contain, but in the potential they afford for abolition-
ist regulations to be added. For example, regulations banning
veal crates and sow stalls and tethers have been added as
regulations under the 1968 Act, and a decision prohibiting
cosmetic testing of finished products and the use of wild
caught primates was made under the auspices of the 1986
Act (Radford, 1996).

A related argument espoused by critics of the property
status of animals is that the inability of animal advocates to

gain legal standing under anti-cruelty statutes has meant that it is difficult, albeit not impossible, to assert the interests of animals in the judicial system. For some (for example, Kelch, 1998: 535–7), this is a direct consequence of animals being regarded as private property and not having legal rights. Clearly, animals do not have the right to legal standing, but this is not the same as saying they do not have legal rights. In state and federal criminal laws in the United States, for instance, private citizens do not have the right to sue criminals, and yet we do not want to say that because of this the rights of the victims of crime have been infringed. This is because, as in anti-cruelty statutes, public prosecutors perform the representative role. The fact that anti-cruelty statutes are weak, or that public prosecutors and courts are not interested in animal cruelty cases is one thing, but it is not caused by the lack of a right to legal standing for animals. The existence of legal rights for animals is therefore independent of the issue of standing.

The law might intervene in property rights to protect animals directly or indirectly. In the latter case, the welfare of animals may be improved but only as an indirect consequence of a law designed to benefit humans. The paradigmatic case here is the existence of legal sanctions against you kicking my dog, designed not to protect animals directly but to protect the animal's owner against any unnecessary distress or economic loss. The ethical backdrop to such a view is the assumption that the interests of the animal do not exist or do not matter, and, as we saw in chapter 1, many esteemed names in the history of political thought – Hobbes (1992), Kant (1965), Locke (1988), to name just three – did hold that the only duties we had to animals were indirect ones. There are few thinkers now, however, who would deny that animals are sentient – can feel and, to a certain extent, think – and, as a result, have interests that ought to be taken into account in any moral calculation.

It is argued by some legal scholars that modern animal welfare statutes also tend to have as their main aim the moral improvement of humans rather than a direct concern to protect the interests of animals (Francione, 1996: 133–6; Rollin, 1981: 12–23). This assertion is surely incorrect. It is certainly true that at the time the first anti-cruelty statutes appeared in the nineteenth century, many, but by no means all, legislators and courts did express an anthropocentric purpose for the statutes (Favre and Tsang, 1993). It is difficult now, though, to maintain this position. Most animal protection statutes recognise that animals can be harmed directly. Thus, in most developed countries a plethora of animal welfare statutes and regulations exist whose aim is to limit property rights in order to benefit animals directly. As Tannenbaum (1995: 166) correctly points out, 'if one were to ask legislators, prosecutors, judges, and employees of humane societies . . . they would say, virtually *universally*, that the primary purpose of these laws is to protect animals'.

This error, that the purpose of anticruelty statutes is for human ends, stems, it seems, from the incorrect assumption that because animals are regarded as property they are equivalent to inanimate objects. Thus, Francione (1996: 131–2) compares anticruelty statutes with the protection of historical landmarks the aim of which is to ensure that human enjoyment of this property continues. But, as Wickland (1997: 572) points out, 'Francione assumes more than proves that animals share the same status as any other property'. On the contrary, there are plenty of examples of judicial decisions where animals are regarded as a special type of private property (Kelch, 1998: 537–40).[3] As Tannenbaum (1995: 131) remarks, 'the actual history of the legal concept of property provides *absolutely no support* for the claim that property, "true" property, or property properly speaking is or should be inanimate'. Thus, the whole point of most animal protection legislation is to protect animals against suffering and, by definition, such legislation recognises the fact that animals represent a particular kind of property by virtue of the fact that they are sentient. For example, as Radford (2001: 222) points out, the British Protection of Animals Act (1911):

> establishes the principle that *the owner of an animal has ultimate responsibility for the way in which it is treated.* Ownership therefore incontrovertibly carries with it *a positive, continuing, non-delegable, legal duty to exercise reasonable care and supervision in order to prevent the animal suffering unnecessarily.* (italics in original)

Animal welfare in comparative focus

Support for the judgement that the property status of animals is not incompatible with a considerable degree of animal welfare can be found in the recognition that the welfare of animals is protected more effectively in some countries than others, and yet the property status of animals remains the same. For example, it is widely recognised that animals receive better protection in Britain than the United States (Garner, 1998). If this is so then the property status of animals cannot be a determining factor since animals are regarded as property in both countries.

There are a number of possible reasons for this discrepancy, which are more important than property in explaining animal welfare standards. One crucially important influence on animal welfare decision-making is the balance of power between those interests arrayed against each other in the political arena. The suggestion here, then, is that the animal use industry is much more influential in the United States than in Britain. This is, partly at least related to the political structure and the social attitudes that, to a greater or lesser extent, influence political decisions.

Public opinion has tended to be much more favourably inclined towards animal welfare in Britain than the United States, thereby reducing the influence of the animal use lobby. Moreover, the American political system is much more fragmented than the British system, where a government with a decent-sized majority in the Commons can usually rely on its backbenchers to get its legislation through. Thus the major legislation relating to farm and laboratory animals in Britain was pushed through parliament by governments intent on seeing it reach the statute book. By contrast, because of the numerous access points in the United States, and the competition for power between elements of the federal government, it is much easier for the animal use lobby to obstruct reforms designed to improve the welfare of animals. This has happened in the case of scientific experimentation (Garner, 1998: 202–28) and animal agriculture, where agribusiness interests are able to control the passage of legislation through relevant Congressional committees (Garner, 1998: 139–50).

The different levels of protection afforded to animals in Britain and the United States is also a product of the wider ideological framework existing in both countries. It might be argued here that the ideology of liberalism, or at least a particular version of it, is much more prominent as a guiding set of principles in the United States than in Britain, or any other country for that matter. Classical liberalism puts great emphasis on the removal of constraints from individuals, the best known account being Mill's harm principle whereby, providing that an individual's actions remain self-regarding, they remain legitimate and only when they become other regarding does the state or society have the right to intervene (Mill, 1972). The value or purpose of private property for liberals is that it provides an arena of autonomy for individuals. There has to be a very good reason, then, for intervening to constrain or limit what individuals do with their private property.

Because of the prevailing liberal ideology, then, there is a general reluctance to restrict property rights in the United States. This does not just affect the treatment of animals, of course, but other aspects of American life. The classic case is the unwillingness of successive generations of American politicians to limit the control of guns, whereas, by contrast, the British Parliament quickly outlawed the ownership of handguns little more than a year after one major shooting incident in Dunblane, Scotland in March 1996 (under the 1997 Firearm Act).

Since animals are also regarded as property it might be suggested that there is a greater reluctance in the United States than in Britain to intervene to protect them against their property owners. It may seem from this that altering the property status of animals in the United States, if not Britain, is necessary even to provide a moderate level of animal protection. Even here, though, the reluctance of the legal and political systems to intervene in property rights to protect animals is itself a product of a society that does not give the welfare of animals a very high priority. In other words, it is not the property status of animals that is ultimately the main problem, as opposed to a disinterested public, and a political system dominated by economic interests which stand to lose in the event of tighter and more stringent animal protection legislation. It is important to note that the predominance of social and political practices over the law is explicit in Britain. It is the common law which includes the right of an animal's owner to dispose of his property in any way he or she sees fit, but this can be overridden by statute law. Thus, the fact that the moral claims of an animal's right to life 'have . . . made no impact whatsoever on either English or Scottish law' (Radford, 2001: 336) is indicative of a lack of social and political will rather than a restrictive set of legal principles.[4]

The importance attached to individual autonomy and self-reliance against the interference of the state and society in the United States, then, is reflected in stringent property laws. It is equally the case that attempts to enforce anti-cruelty statutes, which exist in most American states, are hindered significantly by the weight attached to property rights, and the general assumption that there has to be good reason for interference in property rights makes general legislative improvements in animal welfare difficult (Francione, 1995: 142–56). By contrast, in Britain, it might be suggested, the ideology of individual autonomy and self-reliance has been much less powerful. As Dworkin (1996: 14) points out, in the absence of a formal system of protecting rights in Britain, 'the majoritarian premise has been thought to entail that the community should defer to the majority's view about what . . . individual rights are', and there is a majority view in Britain that the protection of individual rights do not stretch to the right of humans to abuse their animal property as they see fit.[5] Having said that, as we shall see in chapter 3, even in Britain the version of liberal ideology discussed above has undoubtedly had an impact, to the detriment of animal well-being.

It is worth emphasising what is being argued here. It is not so much the existence of stringent property rights that *explains* the relatively poor animal welfare record in the United States. Rather, it is the fact that animals are regarded as insufficiently important to be included within a Mill type harm principle within which their interests would sometimes prevail. Where they are so included, it becomes illegitimate in some cases to exploit animals on liberal grounds because to do so is to act in an other-regarding fashion by depriving them of liberty or even life, or causing them to suffer. This applies whether or not animals are regarded as the property of humans.

Conclusion

The aim of this chapter has been to make a contribution to the debate about the legal status of animals. It has been suggested that the case for moderating or abolishing the property status of animals has been exaggerated. It is neither a sufficient nor necessary step towards a relatively high level of protection for animals. It is not a sufficient guarantee of animal liberation because animals not regarded as property have been shown to be vulnerable to exploitation, because proclaiming rights does not necessarily mean they will be upheld in practice, and because the individualistic language of rights, as we shall discuss further in chapter 5, may not be the most suitable vehicle to ensure the protection of animals subject to institutional exploitation in factory farms and laboratories.

It *is* the case that animals cannot have the full panoply of rights while they remain the property of humans. However, it was also suggested that, all things being equal, it is not necessary to abolish this property status in order to ensure a high degree of animal protection. In other words, animal rights may be incompatible with the ownership of animals, but a useful and viable version of animal welfare need not be. In liberal societies, the viability of animal welfare will depend, as is discussed in the next chapter, upon the degree to which it is recognized that animals ought to be incorporated as beneficiaries of a liberal theory of justice. For now, it is only necessary to note that it is possible to chip away at the property rights of the owners of animals, and envisage a future where the property status of animals is deemed unacceptable. Crucially, though, at that point it will be unnecessary to formally abolish the property status of animals because legislative activity will already have made it redundant.

Further support for the main arguments in this chapter came from a comparative analysis, which showed that it is not the property status of animals that accounts for the differential animal welfare achievements in, for example, Britain and the United States. Instead we have to look elsewhere for explanatory variables. Here, it would seem plausible to suggest that differential animal protection achievements can be at least partly explained by the impact of the political process involving the interaction between interested groups and public opinion. An additional factor is the prevailing ideological climate. More specifically, it is a major contention of this book that a version of liberalism prominent in the West, and particularly the United States, seriously compromises the welfare of animals. It is to a consideration of this prominent version of liberalism that we now turn.

Notes

1 In this context, mention should be made of the decision of the German legislature to grant constitutional rights to animals. The inclusion of animals in the constitution will have to be taken into account by parliament when framing new laws and by the officials and judges who interpret existing legislation. What this means in practice is unclear, but what is clear is that the 'rights' granted to animals are not regarded as the inalienable ones as understood by political and moral philosophers when they talk about the unaquired rights possessed by humans. A better description might be 'interests' since the intention is that the interests of animals in not suffering and being killed will have to be weighed up against the interests of humans in exploiting them. What the new constitutional provision seems to do, therefore, is to officially enshrine animal welfare as a state objective. This is no bad thing but it does not amount to a genuine charter of animal rights that would satisfy animal rights activists (see *Guardian*, 18 May 2002).

2 For example, the U.S. Supreme Court in Scott v. Sanford (1856) held that 'Negroes' were 'property' and not 'citizens'. On the parallels between human and animal subjugation, see Spiegel (1996).

3 Such cases include Corso v. Crawford Dog and Cat Hosp., Inc., 415 N.Y.S. 2d 182, 183, New York Civil Court 1979 where the judge said that 'A pet is not just a thing but occupies a special place somewhere in between a person and a piece of personal property'; Bueckner v. Hamel, 886 S.W. 2d 368, 378, Texas App. Court 1994 where the judge ruled that 'A dog is not a thing ... and to say so is a repudiation of our humaneness'; Katsaris v. Cook, 180 California App. Court, 3d 256, 270, 1986, where it was ruled that 'Not only is a dog more than property today, he is the subject of sonnets, the object of song, the symbol of loyalty. Indeed, he is man's best friend.'

4 Of course, as was pointed out earlier, there is much animal welfare legislation that infringes the ways in which property owners treat their animals. The only instance in which common law has been usurped in life and death issues is where to keep a fatally injured or terminally ill

animal alive is detrimental to its welfare. In these circumstances, 'the law may therefore regard the animal's interest in having its suffering terminated as overriding the owner's property rights' (Radford, 2001: 336–7).

5 The incorporation of the European Convention on human rights into British law may reduce the flexibility traditionally available to British decision-makers. As Radford (2001: 161–2) points out the First Protocol of the Convention emphasizes the autonomy of property owners. The pro-hunting community has already sought to claim that a ban would infringe the Human Rights Act, although the Government has denied this.

3

Political liberalism, animals and justice

This chapter focuses on the third strand of the claim that the effective representation of animal interests is problematic from a liberal perspective. In the last chapter it was argued that the human benefits deriving from animal exploitation in liberal democratic societies are such that the granting of a higher moral status for animals is unlikely to become part of the social and political mainstream. We saw too that the key question then becomes what does the moral orthodoxy, or animal welfare perspective, amount to in a liberal framework. Here, in the second strand, the impact of animals remaining the property of humans was considered. It was suggested that the property status of animals, whilst inimical to the achievement of an animal rights agenda, does not obstruct the achievement of a relatively high level of protection for animals. Instead, it is necessary to look at wider political and ideological factors. This chapter focuses on a central feature of liberal ideology which, it is suggested, impacts negatively on the well-being of animals.

The central feature of liberal political thought, referred to above, is the idea of moral pluralism. Taken to its logical extreme, this principle has traditionally held that the state should not contemplate interfering with individual moral codes or conceptions of the good life until actions deriving from them seem likely to harm other humans in a direct way. Now, it is conceivable that animals could be added to the equation so that moral pluralism can be limited at the point where it harms the interests of animals. However, as we saw in chapter 1, a number of key liberal thinkers – most notably John Rawls – have also sought to exclude animals from a liberal theory of justice. This does not mean that Rawls and other liberal thinkers think that animals are deserving of no moral consideration. Rather, Rawls makes the distinction between a narrow *political* theory of justice, from which deliberations about animals are excluded, and a wider moral theory, from which such deliberations are not.

For this present author it seems entirely appropriate, and useful, for animals to be subject to principles of justice. The problem for those liberal thinkers who exclude animals from such principles is that their assertion, that animals should be the subject of moral consideration from which we can conclude that they think certain ways of behaving toward them are morally impermissible, sits uneasily with the liberal principle of moral pluralism they seek to promote. According to the principle of moral pluralism, the way in which we treat animals becomes a moral preference rather than an obligation insisted upon by the state. Rawls and other liberal thinkers clearly do not want to hold the view that there should be no constraints on what humans may do to animals, not least because they recognise that such a position would put them at odds with the moral orthodoxy. On the other hand, if they seek to constrain the way in which we treat animals, they are then placing limits upon moral pluralism. Therefore, within the constraints of their insistence upon the importance of moral pluralism, it is difficult to see how they can justify seeking to direct our behaviour as they seek to do in the case of our behaviour towards animals. More pertinently, perhaps, the fact that the principle of moral pluralism has been utilized in the animal welfare debate, to the detriment of animal well-being, is indicative of the problematic relationship between Rawlsian liberalism and animals.

Animals and justice

As we saw in chapter 1, mainstream liberal thinkers do accept that we have some direct duties to animals, thereby confirming the validity of a version of the moral orthodoxy, but many leading liberal political theorists also seek to exclude animals as the kind of beings who can be recipients of justice. Most notably, Rawls also holds the dual view that animals are not part of a theory of justice but part of a broader moral terrain. He makes it clear that he thinks that animal interests ought to be subject to some protection. In *A Sense of Justice*, for instance, he (1963: 302) writes that:

> It does not follow from a person's not being owed the duty of justice that he may be treated in any way that one pleases. We do not normally think of ourselves as owing the duty of justice to animals, but it is certainly wrong to be cruel to them.

In *A Theory of Justice*, similarly, he repeats (1972: 512) the point that 'it is wrong to be cruel to animals . . . The capacity for feelings of pleasure and pain and for the forms of life of which animals are capable clearly impose duties of compassion and humanity in their care.'

Rawls does not therefore reject the case for some animal protection. Rather, he implies that, because animals are not moral persons (because, as we saw in chapter 1, they do not have a conception of their good or a sense of justice) they do not have the same degree of protection as humans. What this lesser degree of protection consists of, however, we are none the wiser, and in particular Rawls does not reveal whether he thinks that the interests of animals should ever take precedence over those of humans. Rawls claims that justice is a much narrower area of inquiry than ethics, and the treatment of animals is an issue that is incorporated within the latter and not the former. Rawls touches upon this in *A Theory of Justice* where he remarks (1972: 512) that 'a conception of justice is but one part of a moral view', but a more detailed account can be found in his other book length study *Political Liberalism*. Here (1993: 12–13) he suggests that a 'political' conception of justice is narrower than a comprehensive view in that it only concerns the basic political structure and not 'all kinds of subjects ranging from the conduct of individuals and personal relations to the organization of society as a whole'. As a result, 'the status of the natural world and our proper relation to it is not a constitutional essential or a basic question of justice', and therefore that 'our conduct towards animals is not regulated by' the principles of justice (1993: 246; 1972: 504). Barry (1995: 77) adopts pretty much the same position when he writes that 'it is ... a great mistake ... to suppose that justice as impartiality is intended to constitute a complete, self-sufficient moral system'.

It is not insignificant that liberal thinkers more sympathetic to the claims of animals tend to be more prepared to advocate applying the language of justice to them. Wissenburg (1993: 9–11) argues, for example, that although humans are more important than animals morally, the sentience of the latter and the concomitant responsibility on us this produces means that 'animals can legitimately be called recipients of distributive justice'. The same view is held by Galston (1980: 125) who argues that animals can be harmed directly and therefore 'they must for some purposes be included within the sphere of justice when distributional problems arise'. Dobson (1998: 190–93) too, thinks that a number of the features of the architecture as well as the grammar of social justice 'seem appropriate for nonhuman animals'. Finally, Nozick (1974: 35), in an impressively tortured passage, at least in contrast to Rawls' unfortunate haste, concludes that: 'Animals count for something. Some higher animals, at least, ought to be given some weight in people's deliberations about what to do.'[1]

These statements, if nothing else, suggest that utilizing the language of justice is beneficial to animals. That most would concur with this sentiment is a product of the widespread acceptance that the concept of justice carries greater moral weight than notions of kindness, mercy and charity. It is commonly regarded as our most politically powerful ethical language, and Rawls' liberal theory of justice is a well-known and popular version of the concept. As Johnson (1976: 127) remarks, 'being owed justice is a natural candidate for cashing out special moral status', and to be excluded from it immediately puts animals at a disadvantage. Dobson (1998: 95) concurs when he writes that, 'obligations born of justice are more binding and less revocable than those born of charity'.[2] Finally, to labour the point somewhat, Midgley (1983: 50) gives her assent to the importance of justice by arguing that 'everything outside it begins to look slight and optional'. Significantly, for the present argument, she adds that: 'The boundary of justice becomes that of morality itself. Duties like mercy and compassion then begin to seem like mere matters of taste, aesthetic preferences, luxuries, delightful and desirable no doubt in times of leisure, but not serious.'

It is one thing revealing how animals might benefit from justice, though, quite another to show how they might be worthy recipients of it. There is a strong case, in my view, for the claim that animals should be such recepients. Justice is commonly associated with the distribution of benefits, rewards and duties. Now, while animals cannot be assigned duties, neither can marginal humans who Rawls wants to include as beneficiaries of justice. Moreover, it is accepted by Rawls, Barry and others that animals have interests, a welfare that can be harmed or upheld by the actions of others, and the capacity to experience pleasure or pain as a result of these actions. Even if we accept that the interests of humans take precedence because of their greater capacities, it seems entirely appropriate to include the interests of animals within the justice equation. To do otherwise implies a qualitative difference between humans and animals that the evidence suggests does not exist.

Rawls is entitled, of course, to make the distinction between the realm of justice and the realm of morality because he can still, all things being equal, uphold his commitment to avoiding animal cruelty. All things are not equal, however, since there are two elements specific to Rawls's liberal theory of justice that can be employed to challenge this commitment. The first derives from the particular arrangement of the original position. Without a thickening of the veil to exclude knowledge of species membership, the participants in the original position know they will be humans when the veil is lifted. As a result, there is absolutely no incentive for them to consider the interests of animals at all. As a result, even though this is not his intention, without the incorporation of animals Rawls' theory of justice provides a justification for their ceaseless exploitation, thereby negating the claim that we have some moral duties towards them. Animals are regarded merely as the resources of those who are participants in the original position, and given these participants cannot act altruistically 'except insofar as it is in their self-interest to do it' (Pritchard and Robinson, 1981: 57), the only occasions upon which animals will be protected is as an indirect result of serving some human interest.

Liberalism, the right and the good

The second, and much more important, problematic element of the theory of justice associated with Rawls and
others, as it relates to animals, concerns the central liberal
principle of moral pluralism. It is important to note, firstly,
that there is no reason why animals cannot be incorporated
into a liberal theory of justice. Indeed, as we have seen,
more often than not the case for an elevated moral status
for animals has been made from *within* the liberal tradition, through rights-, utilitarian- or contractarian-based
approaches. Under the auspices of the rights-based approach
it is possible to envisage some version of Mill's harm principle applying, whereby humans are free to do as they wish
provided their behaviour does not harm other humans *and*
animals. Similarly, if the moral orthodoxy is adopted, animals can be protected against unnecessary suffering by invoking the same liberal principle with an adjustment
whereby humans are permitted to harm animals only when
some significant benefit accrues to humans or other animals.

Mill's harm principle, of course, only applies to animals
if they are explicitly incorporated into the theory. Rawls
and other liberal thinkers, as we have seen, fail to do so,
denying responsibility for developing a set of principles by
which our treatment of animals can be judged. As we saw
too, however, these thinkers do think that it matters that
animals are treated humanely. By suggesting that our
treatment of animals belongs to the sphere of morality,
however, such liberal thinkers inadvertently subject them
to the liberal principle of moral pluralism, whereby the
way in which they are treated becomes a matter of personal
preference rather than moral obligation.

The principle of moral pluralism has been described by
Bellamy (1992: 219) as 'the defining political characteristic
of liberalism', an idea which, for Norman Barry (2000: 17),
'has become indissolubly associated with almost all forms
of liberalism', and versions of which can be traced back
through Mill, back to Kant and Locke (Waldron, 1989: 61).
It is a principle which suggests that the liberal state should
observe a neutral stance when faced with competing conceptions of the good. The aim of liberal political theory,
then, is to find, as Plant (1991: 77) points out, 'a set of

rules to guide political action which are independent of a conception of the good'. Thus, any genuine liberal political theory, whether from the classical or egalitarian schools, must include an anti-perfectionist principle of moral pluralism. This is the idea, derived from a wider theory of liberty, that it is no business of the state to interfere in individual moral codes or individual conceptions of the good life. By contrast, a perfectionist theory holds that 'the purpose of the state is to affirm and aid its citizens in seeking the realization of some idea of the good' (Neal, 1997: 4).

A liberal society's function, then, Arblaster (1984: 45) suggests, 'is to serve individuals, and one of the ways in which it should do this is by respecting their autonomy, and not trespassing on their rights to do as they please as long as they can do so without harm to others'. As a result, a liberal state is one that is based on protecting individual rights rather than pursuing certain goals or goods to which the individual must be subsumed. As Mulhall and Swift (1992: 30) elaborate: 'The rights which people have, and which it is the job of the state to protect, come first and stand as constraints on the conceptions of the good which people can choose to pursue.' For Barry (1995: 77), this liberal view defines 'justice as impartiality', which 'is not designed to tell us how to live' but rather 'how are we to live *together*, given that we have different ideas about how to live'. Rawls works out his version most fully in *Political Liberalism* (1993: xix–xx, 134) where he points out that: 'Political liberalism does not attack or criticize any reasonable view. As part of this, it does not criticize, much less reject, any particular theory of the truth of moral judgments'. 'Which moral judgments are true', he continues 'is not a matter for political liberalism', and the difference between this position and that which holds that 'there is but one such conception' of the good 'to be recognized by all citizens' is 'one of the deepest distinctions between conceptions of justice'.

This basic liberal principle of the neutral state has been the guiding force behind what many would regard as some of the most enlightened post-war British legislation, most notably the reform of the law on homosexuality. Liberal, pro-choice, abortion policy too is based on the principle 'that where issues turn on controversial moral or religious conceptions they can justly be disposed of only in one way: by allowing people to follow their own judgment or conscience' (Barry, 1995: 88). What is more, the assumption is that, for liberals, individual choice in the area of morality cannot be obstructed by majoritarianism. It is for this reason, of course, that liberal polities such as the United States have constitutional devices specifically designed to constrain majority decisions.

It is this apparent neutrality, too, which has led some to claim that liberalism represents a unique kind of ideology. All other ideologies, it is suggested, seek to promote a particular version of the good life. Liberalism, by contrast, stands aside from this conflict of ideas by facilitating a variety of conceptions of the good. It is this toleration which led the poet Robert Frost to remark, with irony, that a liberal is someone who cannot take his own side in an argument (quoted in Nagel, 1987: 215).

There is a variety of justifications that liberals have offered for allowing individuals to pursue their own conceptions of the good (Crowder, 1994: 293–305). The liberty to choose one's own conception of the good life is often regarded as an intrinsic good, a matter of showing equal respect for autonomous agents (Dworkin, 1978; Larmore, 1999). As Sher (1997: 15) points out 'when the state promotes a conception of the good, it channels citizens in directions they have not (yet) chosen, and so preempts their autonomous choices'. For Rawls, allowing individuals to pursue their own conceptions of the good is essential to protect liberty. Thus, in *Justice as Fairness* he writes (1991: 150) that the 'only alternative to a principle of toleration is the autocratic use of state power'. Another classic liberal defence is the utilitarian one whereby liberty is also developmental, leading to greater self-knowledge (we all learn from making mistakes), ultimately aiding social progress. We should not presume, it is argued, that we know all there is to know about living and no alternative lifestyles should be condemned because they are different, or because they are a minority pursuit. As Ackerman (1980: 61) remarks, 'the key to liberalism' is 'the perception that we live in a world where people have given *genuinely* different answers to the question of life's meaning'.

In a less elevated and more pragmatic fashion, scepticism about the ability to ever reach a consensus on the competing claims of different conceptions of the good is at the heart of many justifications for moral pluralism. 'The answer that I wish to defend', Barry (1995: 169) opines in a classic statement of scepticism, 'is that no conception of the good can justifiably be held with a degree of certainty that warrants its imposition on those who reject it'. This could evolve into a relativist view, which holds that, since all morality is subjective, there are no moral truths that the state can affirm (Darwell, 1998: 65–6). Indeed, one effect of the liberal defence of the right over the good is to aid the turning of moral beliefs into a matter of personal preferences, however 'rationally argued', thereby giving support to the emotivist school of moral philosophy which claims that moral arguments have always been about arbitrary personal preferences (Darwell, 1998: 72). There is, for Rawls, an element of political fatalism here too. In his later work, he became preoccupied with the good of political stability, for he recognized (1991: 150) that societies with increasingly 'profound differences in beliefs and conceptions of the good' can only be held together by allowing this diversity to flourish unimpeded. His theory then becomes practically designed to ensure social stability by being agreeable to as many people as possible, a position which is heavily criticized by some commentators (see Kukathas and Pettit, 1990: 139–51).

A key question remains the limits which ought to be imposed on the toleration of competing conceptions of the good. It would seem obvious that there has to be some limitations on what a liberal will accept. As Crowder (1994: 303) points out, despite the association of liberalism with pluralism, the two are not necessarily compatible in the sense that the latter:

> tells us that we must choose but not what to choose. It gives us no reason not to embrace values that have ... illiberal implications. We have no reason, as pluralists, not to prefer order and hierarchy to liberty and equality (see also Baum, 1997).

Barry (1995: 130–2), likewise, argues that autonomy is not equivalent to neutrality between substantive conceptions of the good, since autonomy would rule out those conceptions of the good that did not lead to autonomy. We are not free, to put it crudely, to sell ourselves into slavery. At the risk of labouring the point, Larmore (1999: 608) concurs by arguing that, because respect for persons 'lies at the heart of political liberalism . . . it cannot coherently claim to be freestanding with respect to morality altogether'.

Liberals will usually accept some version of Mill's harm principle, and Rawls is no exception since he (1993: 201) adopts what he calls a 'reasonable pluralism'. So, while liberalism 'accepts the plurality of incommensurable conceptions of the good as a fact of modern democratic culture', it is crucial that 'these conceptions respect the limits specified by the appropriate principles of justice' (Rawls, 1991: 164). In other words, the principles of justice 'limit the conceptions of the good which are permissible' [ibid.: 165] and, as a consequence, some moral and political questions can be 'removed from the political agenda' (Rawls, 1993: 151).

Rawls, then, wants to rule out those doctrines and conceptions of the good life which are 'in direct conflict with the principles of justice' and, in particular, those 'requiring the repression or degradation of certain persons on, say, racial, or ethnic, or perfectionist grounds' (Rawls, 1993: 195–6). There is, for instance, a section in his *Political Liberalism* (1993: 151–52, 161) discussing why slavery is unacceptable. However, this detailed account of what conceptions of the good life can be permitted in a liberal society does not sit well with the distinction, noted earlier, Rawls (*ibid.*: 12–13) makes between a 'political' conception of justice which concerns the basic political structure, and a comprehensive account which covers 'all kinds of subjects ranging from the conduct of individuals and personal relations to the organization of society as a whole'. As Moller Okin (1993: 1011) points out 'it seems that though he frequently denies it' Rawls '*is* arguing that persons in the just society should order their whole lives – not only the political aspects of them – in accordance with justice'. Rawls (1993: 152) comments, for instance, that 'does anyone doubt . . . it is wrong to have abolished slavery'. The answer is of course not, but such a view surely presupposes the validity of certain moral principles which, in turn, we are entitled to extrapolate to the case of nonhuman animals.[3] To fail to do so is to make an apparently arbitrary decision to exclude consideration of animals.

The discussion concerning the limits of liberalism's toleration of pluralism has led a number of critics, from within and outside the liberal tradition, to suggest that it is unhelpful, at the very least, to persist with the claim that liberal ideology can be neutral about the good, since it is not itself neutral. Galston (1982: 621), for one, argues very strongly that the theory of liberal neutrality is 'fundamentally misguided' since:

> No form of political life can be justified without some view of what is good for individuals. In practice, liberal theorists covertly employ theories of the good. But their insistence that they do not reduces the rigor of their theories and leaves the liberal polity unnecessarily vulnerable to criticism. (See also Beiner, 1992 and Neal, 1997)

Thus, it is suggested that liberals should seek to justify their own conception of the good rather than deny having one, enabling them to mount an attack on their fiercest critics. Liberals, for instance, are surely opposed to the communitarian emphasis on a communal conception of the good life that may involve the imposition of shared values. To make this attack stick, however, necessitates the revelation that liberals are 'biased towards an individualistic account of human fulfilment' (Waldron, 1989: 79), a claim that genuinely neutral liberals would have to deny. Equally, of course, neutrality is criticized by advocates of the communitarian tradition because while liberals maintain that they are even-handed over competing conceptions of the good they are protected from an attack on the flaws of individualism. Some liberals, most notably Raz (1986), have bitten the bullet and developed a perfectionist version of liberalism. For Raz (1986: 265) 'personal political freedom' is regarded 'as an aspect of the good life', whereas for Neal (1997: 6), similarly, 'autonomy is in fact the good to which contemporary liberalism is fundamentally committed'.

Moral pluralism and animals

For our purpose, it should be emphasized that from the perspective of animal protection, the exclusion of animals from a theory of justice, and therefore a version of the harm principle, is problematic. It is possible to conceptualize harm in a wide sense to include different conceptions of morality, so that I can be harmed by my distaste or disapproval of someone's behaviour. However, this was not Mill's intent and, indeed, it is a liberal article of faith that moral disgust or disapproval, however deeply felt, does not count as harm for the purposes of state or societal intervention. The classic example here, which ironically involves the eating of animals, is Mill's insistence that even in a society where Muslims are in the vast majority, it still remains illegitimate to impose the majority's moral code and forbid the eating of pork (Mill, 1972: 142). In this case, for Mill, the 'only tenable ground of condemnation would be that with the personal tastes and self-regarding concerns of individuals the public has no business to interfere'.

As a result of excluding the impact of morals from the harm principle, animals then become subject to the liberal insistence on moral pluralism, whereby competing moral outlooks are permitted, provided of course they do not harm humans. Treating animals with respect then becomes merely a preference rather than a fundamental principle of justice. In other words, to give an example, *you* may choose to cook lobsters by throwing them alive into pans of boiling water but my moral sensibilities are such that I am not prepared to do this. The state, in addition, is not encouraged to intervene in order to impose my morality on you. Liberal thinkers such as Rawls might, of course, object to the above example on the grounds that it is not a compassionate thing to do, but if we prohibit it on such grounds what becomes of the principle of moral pluralism? Rawls would argue no doubt that he is not advocating a pure version of moral pluralism but one which seeks to constrain behaviour in certain ways. If this is the case, then surely the onus is on him to explain why it is justifiable to limit morality in some ways rather than others and, in particular, why and in what ways it is permissible to limit what can be done to animals.

We saw earlier that there is a debate within liberal political theory about what constitutes a valid conception of the good. Should all tastes and preferences be protected and can and should the state really maintain neutrality as regards competing conceptions of the good? Clearly, as we have seen, it is widely accepted that those conceptions of the good which sanction serious harm to other humans are illegitimate, and this, of course, is why we think, for instance, that 'the conduct of the recreational drug user differs fundamentally from that of the murderer or rapist' (Husak, 2000: 55). This does not help animals much, of course, if the harm principle does not apply to them. Only when the exploitation of animals causes harm to other humans can such activity be prohibited. This helps to explain why defending animal interests as an indirect consequence of protecting human interests is a fertile strategy for the animal protection movement. It is indicative of the dominance of anthropocentrism and the state's reluctance to intervene to protect the interests of animals. In other words, it is much easier to campaign for an animal welfare objective when there will be a human benefit too. There are, for instance, significant environmental and public health implications of factory farming. Similarly, the use of animals in medical research has been criticized as potentially dangerous for humans because animals do not, it is suggested, always make very good models for the treatment of human diseases (Sharpe, 1998).

The question still remains whether there should be any limits on the pursuit of tastes and preferences which fall short of harming humans. In the case of animals Rawls and other liberal thinkers would seem to suggest that there should, although they do not see this as a matter of justice. However, such a position is subject to the critique, mentioned above, that constraining behaviour on compassionate grounds – which the state in most liberal democracies surely does in the case of the welfare of animals – sits uneasily with the principle of moral pluralism. Dworkin remains more consistent here by arguing that there should be no limitation on what we should regard as valid conceptions of the good, providing of course humans are not harmed in the process (see Sinopoli, 1993: 653–5). If watching television and beer drinking are regarded as conceptions of the good, as Dworkin thinks, then why not torturing animals for fun? (Dworkin, 1978).

Limiting tastes, though, is fraught with difficulty, since accusations of paternalism and the illegitimate imposition of favoured conceptions of the good are likely to follow. One possible limitation, which may benefit animals, is that only those tastes and preferences which are authentic should be permitted (Husak, 2000: 53). In other words, those tastes and preferences that are manufactured, say by advertising, are ruled out on the grounds that they have created artificial needs. This is relevant to the welfare of animals in the sense that, for example, the meat industry spends a considerable amount of money painting the production of meat products in the most favourable light possible. Arguably, then, the cruelties of much intensive animal husbandry and slaughter is disguised from the consumer and therefore their choice to eat such products is not as informed as it might be. In other words, the implication here is that if abattoirs had glass walls there would be many more vegetarians.

There are, as one would expect, a number of competing interpretations of this liberal principle of state neutrality. One of the most cited distinctions is the one Raz (1986: 134–6) makes between two anti-perfectionist doctrines, 'neutrality between ideals', and the 'exclusion of ideals'. In the former case, governments are expected to be 'even-handed between all rival moralities' whereas in the latter governments are forbidden to reach decisions on the basis of morality, or at least that part of morality that includes conceptions of the good. The latter would seem to be more consistent with liberal neutrality, and for animals, as we have seen, it is a principle detrimental to the protection of their interests. The promotion by the state of animal welfare is closer to neutrality between ideals although it does not represent even handedness because human interests are given priority.

Brian Barry (1995: 145–51) seeks to rescue liberalism from this conclusion by suggesting that it is consistent in a liberal theory of justice for the state or, more accurately, the people to choose one conception of the good over another providing a democratic procedure has been followed. Barry considers the example, drawn from the famous American case, of a building of a dam, the consequence of which would be the extinction of a species of fish, the snail darter. In the process of deciding whether the dam should be built, Barry thinks it justifiable for individuals to 'appeal to your own conception of the good and try to convince others of your case on the basis of that' (1995: 151). If you hold a conception of the good which includes the preservation of the snail darter and the democratic decision goes against you and the dam is built you can continue to argue the decision was wrong and regrettable. Provided the procedure was just, however, under the terms of justice as impartiality, then the decision is 'legitimate but bad' (1995: 150).

Barry appears to offer a way out of the difficulty of reconciling moral pluralism with a moral imperative to treat animals humanely, since it would seem justifiable for the good of animal protection to be pursued by the state through the mechanism of a democratic procedure, even though by so doing competing conceptions of the good might be damaged in the process. For example, a liberal state could override the interests of those who seek to preserve fox hunting as part of a perceived rural good life, by imposing the competing good of those who think that hunting is cruel and barbaric, provided that the decision was reached by a democratic procedure.

The problem with Barry's argument, however, is that putting competing conceptions of the good to the vote must surely be a last resort for liberals since to do so offends against moral pluralism. Clearly in some cases – Barry's dam is one example – a decision has to be taken one way or the other. Where such a decision can be avoided, though, a commitment to moral pluralism surely necessitates inaction. As Arneson (2000: 66) points out the following of fair procedures 'cannot be an adequate answer to someone who complains that she is unfairly disadvantaged by sectarian state policy'. It is by no means clear that the treatment of animals is an area where decisions are necessary. Indeed, arguments are made against making decisions which seek to promote animal welfare – on ritual slaughter and hunting for instance – precisely on the grounds that to do so would illegitimately subject alternative conceptions of the good to majoritarianism (see below).

Moral pluralism in practice

Put in the context of our relationship to nonhuman animals the principle of moral pluralism and the neutral state means, as Clark (1987: 121) asserts, that 'third parties have no right to come between the whaler and her prey, or the farmer and her veal calves, since none of us have a right to impose our "merely" moral standards on other autonomous agents'. From this, it is clear that the implications of adopting a position of moral neutrality as far as animals are concerned is surely counter to our moral intuition (and the practices of most liberal democratic polities) which insists on limiting, by statute law, what we are permitted to do to them, whatever our inclinations. This conclusion tends to undermine Rawls' ambition of providing a set of liberal principles which has universal assent.

Examples of the way in which moral pluralism has been detrimental to the protection of animal interests will be provided below. It should also be noted at this point that, together with neutrality in the sense of Raz's exclusion of ideals, the state could adopt three other positions on the relationship between humans and animals. It could regard the claims of humans and animals as equivalent, it could seek to intervene to promote animal welfare or it could intervene to promote, as opposed to allowing to continue, those activities which involve the exploitation of animals. Allowing animal exploitation to continue unchecked is, of course, not the same as neutrality, but is arguably more beneficial, or less harmful, to animals than the active promotion of animal exploitation. The American philosopher Bernard Rollin illustrates the biased nature of the state's inactivity in relating a conversation with a prominent medical researcher in which he was told that 'morality is a matter of taste in a free country', and that Rollin was entitled to his opinion but ought not to impose it on others. Rollin responded by saying that the absence of constraints on the use of animals in research meant that the medical researcher was imposing *his* morality on him (quoted in Gluck *et al.*, 2002: 118).

The promotion of animal exploitation would make animals worse off than state neutrality. Whilst the promotion of meat eating and animal experimentation by public authorities is not rare, it is much less common to see it coupled with strident criticisms of animal activists and a failure to balance it with recognition of the need to minimise animal suffering. This latter scenario tends to occur more often in the United States than Britain. In 1990, for instance, on the eve of a major demonstration in Washington DC by animal protection activists, the Secretary of Health and Human Services, Louis Sullivan, sought to discredit the animal rights movement by labelling it indiscriminately as terrorist and anti-science. In another instance, an important official in the same department embarked on a major programme of action to defend animal research arguing that:

> I believe that it would be a dereliction of duty were I, as head of a major health agency and as a physician, not to help make the public aware of the true nature of the animal rights movement and to educate them to the health benefits that accrue to them as a consequence of responsible animal research. (Garner, 1998: 216–17)

The more strident attitudes present amongst public officials in the United States should be contrasted with the much more conciliatory nature of British governments. Thus, the Conservative government in the 1980s took inordinate care to try to ensure that they kept 'on board' the moderate faction of the animal protection movement during the passage of the Animals (Scientific Procedures) Act 1986 (Garner, 1998: 182–7). More recently, to give another example, the Labour Government was, at least initially, extremely wary about intervening to protect the beleaguered Huntingdon Life Sciences contract research laboratory, subject to an unremitting campaign by the animal rights movement. Thus, the Government's 'endorsement of the firm's right to continue legitimate research was carefully offset by support for lawful protest' (*Guardian*, 17 January 2001).

As the campaign against Huntingdon intensified, including the undoubted use of intimidatory tactics by animal rights activists, the Government did adopt a tougher attitude towards protestors and greater support for the company, particularly after lobbying from industry groups. Thus, Ministers visited the site and, after the company's financial collapse, provided banking facilities for it too. Nevertheless, despite this, British Governments remain reluctant to appear too one sided in their approach to animal issues. The latest example of this was the apparent snubbing of Colin Blakemore, an Oxford neuroscientist and a noted opponent of the animal rights movement, in the 2003 honours list for fear of 'upsetting' animal activists.

Leaked documents indicated that Blakemore – who, in a rather self-important manner, threatened to resign as head of the Medical Research Council over the issue – was excluded because of his 'controversial' work on vivisection (*Guardian*, 22 December 2003; 13 January 2004). The decision provoked a furious response from many scientists (and contributions from animal advocates too) revealing, among other things, how some members of the scientific community expect the government to be biased in favour of animal research and – rightly or wrongly – regard the Blakemore incident as another indication that they are not. Professor Reichard Naftalin, for instance, wrote that:

> Professor Blakemore is right to claim that withholding recognition from him sleights science. On this issue, he deserves support from all scientists ... If the Prince [of Wales, apparently responsible for blocking an honour to Blakemore] disapproves of vivisection, he can join the anti-vivs. (*Guardian*, 2 December 2003)

Arguably, it is not government perfectionism that is the major disadvantage to animal rights advocates. Rather, meat eating and, to a lesser degree, animal experimentation, are such a dominant part of modern culture that these are practices accepted by most without too much thought. As Adams (1994: 38) remarks:

> In a sense, vegetarians are no more biased than corpse eaters about their choice of food; the former, however, do no benefit as do the latter from having their biases actually approved of by the dominant culture through the coercive effects of a government-sponsored corpse diet.

To see how ingrained meat eating is in our society, it is worthwhile, following Adams (1994: 38), recognizing how odd labelling on meat would look if it was written from a vegetarian's perspective. 'Warning: This is a dead body, recently executed', it might say: 'The decaying process has already begun. You do not need to eat dead animals to stay healthy. Reduce your risk of getting six out of ten diseases that cripple and kill Americans: Boycott this product and choose vegetarianism.'

The above examples reveal that a perfectionist alternative to moral pluralism is not necessarily beneficial to animals, a point to which we shall return in chapter 4. Having

said that, the practical implications for animals of the principle of moral pluralism have, I would argue, been profound.
This is because the moral pluralism argument has been utilized, quite successfully, in practice by those who seek to
exploit animals. There are two classic examples whereby
those who seek to continue exploiting animals explicitly use
the language of liberal moral pluralism to justify and preserve
their activities.

The first of these is hunting with hounds in general, and
fox hunting in particular. Ironically, the image of fox hunting and its supporters is conservative, whereas advocates
of abolition are often perceived as middle-class liberals.
Conservative traditionalism is undoubtedly an important
factor in the support of fox hunting, and yet proponents
have increasingly used the language of liberalism to defend
their activity (Scruton, 2000: 116–22). Faced by an aboli-
tionist majority (in the Commons and, according to most
opinion polls, the general public), the hunting community
has elicited a good deal of sympathy by painting the
opponents of hunting as an illiberal mob intent upon an
attack on a defenceless minority. Thus, the 2002 Countryside Alliance demonstration in London was labelled the
'Liberty and Livelihood' march.

The transformation of the hunting community's case –
from being based on arguments that hunting is a form of
pest control or that it serves an environmental function –
to one centring on liberty has undoubtedly strengthened its
position, not least because it has won it some allies in
the liberal press and academic community (although see an
alternative view from Hutton, 2002). Thus, the late Hugo
Young (1999) could write in the impeccably liberal *Guardian*
that:

> hunting is an issue about the toleration of choice. The ban, if it
> happens, will ask a serious question about Labour's reliability
> as a defender of minorities. It will show New Labour as a party
> of new illiberalism ... At the bottom of the rage to ban
> hunting is the sense that here is a sport engaged in only by a
> minority ... The defining progressive precept, however, should
> be toleration.

Similarly, Roger Scruton (2000: 196) complains, somewhat
oddly given his conservative credentials, that the attempt

to ban hunting 'shows the extent to which old-fashioned liberal principles are now being expelled from the political process'. Neither have Conservative politicians been reticent to jump on the liberty bandwagon. Nicholas Soames, commenting on one of the many anti-hunting bills put before parliament since the 1997 General Election, argued that: 'This wicked proposal would separate liberty from justice and is a thoroughly undesirable thing to do.' John Gummer, similarly, commented that: 'This is a serious matter ... about freedom which, if it is carried through, will threaten every minority in this country' (*Guardian*, 21 December 2000).

The second example of the conflict between moral pluralism and animal welfare concerns the issue of ritual slaughter. In many countries, including Britain but not Switzerland, Norway, Sweden or Ireland, ritual slaughter practised by Jewish and Muslim communities, which involves killing the animals without pre-stunning, is permitted. In Britain, stunning has been required – for cattle, sheep, goats, swine and horses – by national legislation since the 1933 Slaughter of Animals Act, updated by the 1974 Slaughterhouses Act, and for poultry by the 1967 Slaughter of Poultry Act. All of these pieces of legislation contain exemptions for the Jewish practice of Shechita, and the similar Muslim practice of Dhabh, whereby, on religious grounds, animals and birds killed for food must not have suffered any injury before slaughter if the meat produced is to be kosher (for Jews) and halal (for Muslims). Similarly, EU law excludes ritual slaughter from the general stunning requirement (Radford, 2001: 117).

There is significant evidence that ritual slaughter represents a severe welfare problem. The practice involves the cutting of an animal's throat with a sharp knife without pre-stunning, which means that the animal remains conscious for 'an unacceptably long' period 'during which', according to experts in the science of animal welfare, 'the animal must be in great pain and distress' (FAWC, 1985: 20; Fraser and Broom, 1990: 152). Moreover, additional welfare problems are created by the *way* in which animals are ritually slaughtered. Some animals in the United States, for instance, are shackled and hoisted – as stunned animals are – before having their throats cut while fully conscious

(Singer, 1990: 154). A British government report also revealed that a substantial proportion – up to two thirds – of
meat produced by ritual slaughter is made available on the
general market with no indication of its origins (FAWC,
1985: 8–9). There is still no statutory requirement to label
such meat, although it is an offence to knowingly sell meat
produced by ritual slaughter not for the food of Muslims or
Jews, and such a situation is clearly counter to the liberal
emphasis on choice.

Over the years in Britain ritual slaughter has been
opposed by a variety of official committees, most notably
by the government-appointed Farm Animal Welfare Council
(FAWC, 1985, 2003), as well as the EU's Scientific Veter-
inary Committee which recommended to the European
Parliament in 1990 that legal exemptions to pre-stunning
be abolished (Poulter, 1998: 139). Moreover, it has also been
opposed by the animal welfare community, and a total of
six Private Members Bills were introduced between 1955
and 1998 with the aim of removing the exemption, and a
large majority of public opinion has been against the practice (Poulter, 1998: 133–8).[4] And yet ritual slaughter has
survived, and it has survived because of the employment
of liberal notions of moral pluralism and religious toleration. Thus, the British Government has refused to ban
the exemption on the grounds that it 'recognizes a fundamental matter of religious belief to communities that are
an important part of our national life' (HC Debs, 2 February
1997, col 659). As Aitkenhead (2003) reports: 'Nobody
seriously expects the Government to change the law. They
all agree it would be politically untenable'. Significantly,
all of the broadsheet newspapers, in the light of the Farm
Animal Welfare Council's most recent report calling for an
end to religious slaughter (2003), defended it on the grounds
of religious freedom. The tabloids, surprisingly given their
past record on issues involving race, ignored it completely.

This religious rationale is particularly symbolic given
that the roots of liberal toleration and neutrality lie in the
need to reconcile a Europe riven by religious conflicts at
the time of the Protestant Reformation (Barry, 2001: 21,
25). Significantly, Article 9 of the European Convention on
Human Rights, now incorporated into British law in the

1998 Human Rights Act, recognizes religious freedom, and any future attempt at an EU or British government level to end ritual slaughter is likely to conflict with this provision (Radford, 2001: 117). It is difficult to think of a scenario more in keeping with key liberal principles than this.

Barry (2001: 39–43) argues that because of the evidence that animals suffer as a result of ritual slaughter, it is a practice which is 'virtually impossible to provide an intellectually coherent rationale for', and yet it exists, he claims, because of, what he sees as, the illegitimate influence of multiculturalism rather than liberalism (2001: 295). Thus, ritual slaughter, he argues, is mistakenly regarded as an issue of religious liberty whereas in fact it is a dietary request. Either Jews and Muslims should cease eating meat, he concludes, or, as in countries, such as Norway, Sweden and Switzerland, the religious authorities should declare that the religious order does not have to be followed.[5] Barry also, correctly, notes that ritual slaughter is an example of the 'rule-and-exemption' approach to public policy whereby there is a rule that has to be followed by all except those who raise an objection to it (Barry, 2001: 39). By contrast, at least as presently constituted, hunting is a libertarian issue permitted without exception. Barry sees the rule-and-exemption approach as flawed, and to illustrate this he seeks to apply it to hunting, whereby hunting was banned unless it could be shown in any particular case to be part of the hunter's culture. 'It is implausible', he writes (2001: 43) 'that a fox would feel better about hunting if it knew that it was to be chased by the Duke of Beaufort than if it knew it was to be chased by Roger Scruton, whom it might regard as a parvenu unable to claim hunting as part of his ancestral way of life' just as it 'is hard to see why some cows and sheep should have to suffer in ways that are unacceptable generally in order to enable people with certain religious beliefs to eat their carcasses'.

We can readily agree with Barry's conclusion that the case for ritual slaughter is weak, but the key point for us is the degree to which this case is based on liberal principles. In this author's view, it clearly is. A liberal would not accept Barry's critique of the application of an exemption on religious or cultural grounds, since from a liberal animal welfare perspective it is not the feelings of the animals that takes precedence but the benefits to humans. Thus, on liberal grounds it is quite justifiable to allow a minority to gain the perceived religious benefits that it is claimed derive from ritual slaughter. In short, religious toleration, as we have seen, is an important liberal principle. It is equally plausible, from a liberal perspective, to envisage the rule-and-exemption approach applied to hunting. Indeed, this is exactly what the British Government proposed to Parliament in the summer of 2003, when it suggested that hunting be banned except where it could be shown that it is necessary to reduce the fox population. The fact that utility rather than culture was the rationale in this case, nor the fact that MPs voted against the Government proposals in favour of an outright ban, does not alter the force of the point. The rule-and-exemption approach is consistent with liberalism. Returning to ritual slaughter, finally, even if we accept that Barry is right to say that a law banning ritual slaughter 'does not restrict religious liberty, only the ability to eat meat' (2001: 44), it is the case then that those involved are deprived of the freedom to eat meat, all in the name of an attack on religious autonomy.

It is not only in the two areas discussed above where the idea of moral pluralism has influenced the debate about our treatment of animals. Instead of legislative action prohibiting or regulating what may be done to animals, our behaviour towards them tends in many instances to be governed by a whole series of voluntary choices. We are free whether or not to hunt animals, free to abstain from eating meat or not, free to eat free-range or intensively produced animal products. Similarly, we are free to choose to buy cosmetics not tested on animals, even free to choose whether or not to partake of drugs which have been developed through the use of animals, and toxicity tested on them once developed.

It is true that a considerable amount of animal welfare legislation now exists, particularly in liberal democratic states in Europe. This reflects our moral intuition that animals ought to be protected by the state. Moreover, the liberal emphasis on choice might seem a civilized way of dealing with inevitable differences of moral opinion. For animal advocates, certainly, the fact that a more genuine choice now exists – in supermarkets and restaurants especially – is an important advance. Nevertheless, the greater choice made available is no substitute for statute law regulating and/or prohibiting certain ways of treating animals. Many of the worst excesses of intensive animal agriculture – battery cages, beak trimming, tail docking, live exportation over long distances and so on – still exist even in a country such as Britain, which is meant to be more enlightened than most on this issue. It cannot be proved that there is a link between the choices available and the relative paucity of statute law, but the existence of the former undoubtedly makes the animal suffering that is still permitted more palatable.

As we pointed out in chapter 2, it is perhaps not insignificant either that in the United States, where liberal ideology plays a much more prominent societal and political role, animals are less well-treated than in many European countries (Garner, 1998). The importance attached to individual autonomy and self-reliance against the interference of the state and society is reflected, firstly, in stringent property laws. As Vincent asserts, 'property is the precondition to the development of the person. To interfere with property is a gross infringement of rights and liberties' (Vincent, 1995: 43). As was found in chapter 3, it is not surprising that attempts to enforce anti-cruelty statutes, which exist in most American states, are hindered significantly by the weight attached to property rights, and the general assumption that there has to be good reason for interference in property rights makes general legislative improvements in animal welfare difficult (Francione, 1995, 1996). By contrast, in Britain, it might be suggested, the ideology of individual autonomy and self-reliance has been much less powerful.

There is another by-product of the liberal emphasis on individual autonomy that is worth mentioning. This relates to its developmental purpose. The traditional justification for restricting society and the state's role in the lives of individuals, as exemplified by Mill's utilitarian analysis, is to promote social progress, a goal consistent with liberalism's traditional emphasis on human mastery of the natural world. As we have seen, the liberal exponents of a higher moral status for animals have been well served by using the kind of rationalistic arguments attractive to liberal opinion.

Ironically, though, if animals are excluded from the protection afforded by rights, which is always the case, then they
are likely to become the victims of the liberal emphasis on
reason, science and progress. This is particularly the case
for animals used in scientific and agricultural research which,
in the new world of biotechnology, has become more extreme and terrifying for animals (see Rollin, 1995, and see
chapter 4 for a discussion of the conservative critique of
this aspect of liberalism).

The impact of moral pluralism on the well-being of
animals then is clear. I might decide to desist from activities which exploit animals, and my moral choice will be
respected or at least tolerated. Equally, though, since this is
about moral choice, other individuals are entitled to hold
contrary preferences, and, although I am entitled to try to
persuade them to change their minds, I am expected to
respect their preferences, and not obstruct their pursuit of
them, even if I fundamentally disagree with them. In this
context, contrast vegetarianism with the modern attitude
most have to smoking. Whereas a group of vegetarians in a
restaurant cannot expect that meat eating be prohibited
within their eye-range, there is every likelihood that smoking will be prevented where people are eating. This distinction
comes about, of course, as a result of the fact that smoking
in a populated environment is defined as an other-regarding
activity, because of the alleged effects of passive smoking,
whereas my moral repugnance at your meat-eating is not
similarly regarded.[6]

Crucially, although it might be argued that it is the duty
of the liberal state to make its citizens aware of the full
range of moral beliefs available, including those which argue for the protection of animals, the state must ultimately
desist – Barry's arguments discussed above permitting –
from intervening to favour one set of moral beliefs over
another. In other words, as Macintyre (1988: 336) points
out: 'Every individual is to be equally free to propose and to
live by whatever conception of the good he or she pleases
... unless that conception of the good involves reshaping
the life of the rest of the community in accordance with it.'
Whether or not the state should intervene to impose a moral
code that, for instance, makes vegetarianism compulsory
is, of course, a big question which is beyond the scope of

this chapter. What is undoubtedly true, however, is that an ethic based on moral pluralism makes it much more difficult for *any* kind of restrictions on the way humans treat animals to be introduced. Even Rawls would be unwilling to accept this as a satisfactory state of affairs.

Conclusion

Liberalism can be rescued from the charge that it is an apologist for animal suffering, but this can only happen if animals are included, along with humans, among those entities that we are obliged to protect as a matter of justice. At this point, it becomes illegitimate to exploit animals on liberal grounds because to do so is to act in an other-regarding fashion by depriving them of liberty or even life, or causing them to suffer. Animals can be incorporated within a liberal theory of justice whether they are granted an inferior moral status to humans (the moral orthodoxy) or whether they are granted a moral status more or less equivalent to humans (an animal rights or liberation position). As we saw in chapter 1, there is a strong case for the latter verdict, although it was also suggested in chapter 2 that there are various practical reasons why such an eventuality is unlikely.

A number of mainstream liberal political theorists including Rawls, however, insist that justice cannot apply to animals. The resulting exclusion and marginalization of animal interests is regrettable, since, whilst these thinkers are equally insistent that animals do have some moral weight, although clearly not as much as humans, they fail to see the difficulty of reconciling moral strictures about the need to be compassionate to animals with their strongly-held advocacy of moral pluralism, a principle which can, and has in practice, been utilized to justify animal exploitation. The problematic nature of the relationship between liberalism and the protection of animals, highlighted in particular in Rawls' theory, means that we should consider looking elsewhere in a search for the most appropriate ideological location for the protection of animal interests. The next four chapters attempt this task.

Notes

1 Nozick did not have the benefit of much of the modern animal ethics literature when he was writing *Anarchy, State and Utopia*, although he does (1974: 338) indicate the he read an early work by Singer after his comments on animals were written. As Dobson (1998: 174) comments:

> One wonders what Nozick's theory of justice would have looked like had he (Nozick) been armed with Singer's fully worked out theory of animal liberation, and also with Tom Regan's case for animal rights. It is tempting to surmise that if Nozick had prepared his text a few years later, then his would have been the only major theory of intra-human justice to have emerged from contemporary Western political theory which systematically incorporated obligations of justice to (some) sentient beings as well.

2 Not all schools of thought, it should be noted, accept this view. Most importantly, as chapter 7 will reveal, a central plank of the feminist case for animal protection is those traditional justice-based attempts to justify a higher moral status for animals are flawed because they rely on arguments based upon rationality, logical consistency, and fairness which are always going to advantage humans over animals. Instead, feminists argue, these essentially male arguments should be replaced by a 'care ethic' which privileges essentially female values such as compassion, empathy and sympathy that constitutes a much more appropriate language for animal advocates than rationality and justice.

3 See Spiegal's (1988) book which explicitly draws a comparison between the treatment of animals and human slavery.

4 A contrary view is expressed by Poulter (1998: 138–41). In the context of the present discussion, though, the pros and cons of ritual slaughter are secondary to the utilization of liberal ideas in its defence.

5 Investigative journalism has revealed that in Britain most slaughter-houses claiming to provide halal meat are in fact pre-stunning animals, in full knowledge of the Halal Food Authority, on the grounds that it is easier and less cruel (Aitkenhead, 2003). Ironically, now this has come to light there has been pressure on slaughterhouses by Muslim authorities to ensure that ritual slaughter is carried out properly in the future.

6 It is possible, short of including animals as beings subject to the other-regarding principle, to protect them from harm but only if we invoke the indirect duties view, explained in chapter 1, whereby, for instance, the infliction of violence towards animals might precipitate violence towards humans. This is not the place to explore this link, although there is empirical evidence for it (Adams, 1995). Such an approach is, for most though, illegitimate, insofar as it fails to recognize that animals can be harmed directly.

4

Conservatism, communitarianism and animals

We begin our exploration of the fit between non-liberal political ideologies and animal protection by examining the claims of conservatism and communitarianism. In some ways, conservatism and communitarianism, particularly in the sense that they share a non-individualistic vision of society, are similar. Both certainly offer answers, however plausible, to the liberal weaknesses, at least as far as the protection of animals is concerned, we have identified in the preceding two chapters. Indeed, communitarianism, at least in its modern form, derives much of its impetus as a response to the renewed liberal emphasis on the priority of the right over the good exemplified in the work of Rawls.

Both conservatism and communitarianism have some claim to be appropriate ideological locations for the protection of animals. The emphasis in the former on tradition and the attack on human attempts at mastery over nature has a great deal of resonance in a critique of modern animal agriculture and experimentation. Likewise, with its emphasis on a shared conception of a good life promoted by a perfectionist state, communitarianism minimises the problems for animals of the liberal insistence on moral pluralism and state neutrality, concepts which are, as we shall see, open to criticism independently of their impact upon the interests of animals. Ultimately, though, neither ideology provides an adequate grounding for animal interests. With honourable exceptions, thinkers in both ideological traditions remain anthropocentric. The most that can be hoped for from conservatism is a commitment to some level of animal welfare, whilst the inherent conservatism of at least some communitarian writing, coupled with an opposition to universal principles of justice, means that even this might be asking too much.

Conservatism

Whilst there is no one coherent account of conservative prescriptions towards animals, familiar themes within conservative thought can be utilized in their favour. The major exponent here is John Gray (2002) who, writing in a classic Burkean idiom, ridicules the view that humans are masters of their own destiny. As a result, humans are little different from animals. Despite the humanist belief that humans are special by virtue of being self-conscious and capable of exercising free-will, we are in fact like other animals having relatively little control over the direction of our lives.

More specifically, Gray condemns the industrialization of farming – 'an industry at the cutting edge of technological intervention in natural processes' – as an ill-founded attempt to control and dominate nature. The resulting crisis in food production – BSE, CJD and salmonella – he sees as inevitable consequences of tampering with a system that we are ill-equipped to understand fully (Gray, 1997: 151). Rather, 'we must respect the natural world on which we depend more and invest fewer of our hopes in the project of transforming it by the use of technology' (ibid.: 152).

Scruton (2000: 139) adopts a similar line when he asks us to value piety as 'a confession of ignorance'. Piety, he continues, would have 'caused us to hesitate before feeding to cows, which live and thrive on pasture, the dead remains of their own and other species'. Piety would, in general terms, mean that we would 'hesitate before the mystery of nature, to renounce our presumption of mastery, and to respect the process by which life is made'. A similar critique of enlightenment rationalism can be utilized to challenge the validity of using animals in the increasingly extreme pursuit, now involving genetic engineering, of scientific knowledge (Rollin, 1995). Scruton (2000: 107) himself describes the most extreme procedures, particularly on the higher mammals, as 'callous', but concedes that the 'relentless course of science will always ensure that these experiments occur'. 'But that', he concludes, 'is part of what is wrong with the relentless course of science'.

Conservatives tend to eschew the traditional liberal notions of right and duties to animals in favour of a broader paternalism. This comes across very strongly in an impressively weighty and passionate, albeit somewhat rambling, tome about animals by Matthew Scully (2002: xi–xii), the American conservative (and former special assistant and speechwriter to George W. Bush.). 'Animals are more than ever a test of our character, of mankind's capacity for empathy and for decent, honourable conduct and faithful stewardship', he writes. We should treat them with kindness, he continues: 'not because they have rights or power or some claim to equality, but in a sense because they don't; because they all stand unequal and powerless before us'. And again: 'Human beings love animals as only the higher love the lower, the knowing love the innocent, and the strong love the vulnerable.'

With the honourable exceptions mentioned in the preceding few paragraphs, however, conservatives in general have been dismissive about the moral claims of animals. Even those conservatives who do mention animals only lend support to animal welfare. Conservatism would seem to rule out moral extensionism as a radical project. Thus, Gray, Scruton and Scully may oppose industrialized animal agriculture but would seem to have few problems with a less intensive, and more traditional, approach to animal husbandry (Scruton, 2000: 144–5, 165–72; Scully, 2002: 247–86).

I used the phrase 'would *seem* to have few problems' in the previous paragraph because, shorn of the prescriptions provided by abstract theories, conservative defenders of animals have trouble finding a precise guide to right action. Scully (2002: 24), for instance, in an impeccably conservative fashion, criticises rights and utilitarian approaches because they 'risk pulling animals out of the world where affection and creaturely goodwill are possible'. However, when it comes to replacing this with his own prescription he says (*ibid.*: 24):

One doesn't have to pull them from their place and demand perfect equality to care for them, to see in animals the moral dignity only man can perceive, and to refrain wherever possible from harming them, as only man the rational and moral creature can do.

What constitutes 'wherever possible' we are left to guess at.

Finally, it should also be noted that a focus on tradition can also lead to support for the continuation of practices which exploit animals. The classic case here, of course, is fox hunting in Britain, although similar arguments have been employed in support of the use of animals in fiestas and bull fighting in Spain and in rodeos in the United States. Thus Scruton (2000: 161), although interestingly not Gray, supports hunting on the grounds that it 'is the best that we over-civilised beings can hope for, by way of a homecoming to our natural state'. Gray (1997: 144), by contrast, opposes hunting but, significantly, does so by suggesting that the liberal grounds of defence discussed in the previous chapter has been adopted by the hunting community, despite the fact that they 'despised and ridiculed' it in the past, precisely because 'they perceive – correctly – that they can no longer hope for their pursuits to survive on the basis of any form of social deference'.

Some commentators have tried to draw links between the far right and environmentalism in general and the protection of animals in particular (see Bramwell, 1989). It is true that the Nazis were interested in environmental issues, including animal welfare. For instance, vivisection was restricted, nature reserves were set up and, for at least a period of time too, Hitler and Himmler were vegetarians and the former, in particular, was apparently extremely fond of his pets. Scruton (2000: 86) wants to make a great deal of this. 'It is in no way surprising', he writes:

that Hitler ... sentimentalised animals and lived among pets. The very same man who commanded the murder of six million innocent people and the torture and ruin of millions more, was the first European leader to outlaw hunting, on the grounds that animals are innocent and that to hunt them is cruel. The sentimentalising ... of pets may seem to many to be the epitome of kind-heartedness. In fact it is very often the opposite: a way of enjoying the luxury of warm emotions without the usual cost of feeling them, a way of targeting an innocent victim with simulated love that it lacks the understanding to reject or criticise.

We can dismiss this amateur psychology as irrelevant to the present discussion, which is about any ideological compatibility between animal protection and the far right, although it does serve to illustrate how any such links, however tenuous, are used to slur those with an interest in protecting animal interests. What we can say is that there is some truth in the claim that, as Hay (1988: 23) points out, Green thought shares some of the ideological discourse of fascism in terms of the: 'Use of biological metaphors, stress on the organic community ... elevation of ritual, intuition and the mystical, and distrust of the rational'. Moreover, to continue this theme of association between animal protection and the far right, one of the authors of a major study of the American animal protection movement claimed that anti-Semitism in the movement is common (Jasper and Nelkin, 1992: 47–8, 186).

We should not take the claim that there is a close fit between animal protection and the far right too seriously. For one thing, leaving aside the links between the holism of much Green thinking and fascism, animal rights/ liberation views have at their core respect for individuals, whether they be humans or animals. In fact, the interest that the Nazis had in vegetarianism was little to do with a recognition of the moral significance of animals, and more to do with an anthropocentric concern for the quality of food, which in turn was linked to the ideological emphasis on racial purity (Francione, 2000: 174–5). We should not therefore draw any significant conclusions from the Nazi interest in the protection of animals. As Vincent (1995: 266) remarks, just 'because national socialists used social- ist methods or favoured ancient German traditions does not mean that either socialism or conservatism are eter- nally besmirched'. The same applies to animal protection. There is little evidence, finally, that anti-Semitism is rife in the American animal protection movement as Nelkin claimed. Indeed, her co-author, James Jasper – who, of the two, is the lead researcher on this issue thinks it is rare (Jasper and Nelkin, 1992: 186).

Defining communitarianism

Since the 1970s, communitarianism has provided a more potent ideological challenge to liberalism than conservatism and socialism.[1] Defining the basic thrust of communitarianism is difficult because of the disparate nature of its adherents, coming from the right and left of the political spectrum (both conservatism and socialism, of course, have communal elements), and also because some of those who have been described as communitarians have disputed the label (see, for example, Sandel, 1998: x–xi). The essence of the communitarian approach is an attack on what is perceived to be the asocial individualism of liberalism. This attack is both methodological and normative (Avineri and De-Shalt, 1992: 2).

Methodologically, communitarians argue that human behaviour is best understood in the context of the social, historical and cultural environments of individuals. The pre-social autonomy of the liberal social contract tradition, revived by Rawls, is, for communitarians, a deeply flawed account of the human condition, embodying 'the mistaken view that people's ends are formed independently of or prior to society'. Rather, 'it is the kind of society in which people live that affects their understandings both of themselves and of how they should lead their lives' (Mulhall and Swift, 1996: 13). There is some support, in the communitarian literature, for what Caney (1992: 275) has called the 'wholly embedded' thesis in which individuals are wholly shaped by their community, whereas others advocate the 'partially embedded' thesis which, as the name suggests, enables individuals to distance themselves from community norms. A further, and more extreme, disagreement within the communitarian literature is that some communitarian writing suggests that the basis of the communitarian critique of liberalism is the normative assertion that liberal theory accurately reflects liberal society and therefore ought to be transformed. Others suggest, methodologically, that liberal theory misrepresents the reality of modern societies where social ties are more important in determining the belief-systems of individuals than liberal theory has realized (Walzer: 1990).

What is clear is that, normatively, communitarians emphasise the value of communal existence, and the importance of being bound together by a shared vision of the good promoted by a perfectionist state (Kymlicka, 1990: 205–7), part of a tradition that can be traced back to Aristotle – on which particular emphasis is placed by MacIntyre (1985). This is contrasted with the grim isolation of the 'unencumbered' liberal self (Sandel, 1984). Furthermore, since individuals internalise the values and traditions of their communities, then the search for a universal theory of justice is a forlorn one, and ought to be replaced by a recognition of the importance of particularity. Within this broad framework, there is plenty of scope for very different accounts of the communal life, ranging from traditional hierarchical societies to radical participatory democracies.

Challenging the neutral state

Before we move on to examine specifically the relationship between communitarianism and the protection of animal interests, it is worthwhile exploring the case for communitarianism more generally. Of greatest importance here is a successful critique of the viability of moral pluralism and state neutrality in general, political forms against which communitarians array themselves. A number of points can be made here. In the first place, a critique of the viability of moral pluralism would include an empirical assault on the possibility of its existence. In other words, the state, it might be argued, cannot be neutral. As Neal (1997) comments governments are 'not merely passive receptacles which respond to autonomous demands, interests and preferences arising from society', but 'play quite a significant role in shaping both the form and content of those demands, interests and preferences'. We saw in the previous chapter, for instance, how governments sometimes promote practices which exploit animals, and that arguably, too, state inaction is not itself a neutral act for animals because it implicitly accepts practices which cause animal suffering.

The second challenge to the viability of moral pluralism and state neutrality is a critical analysis of moral scepticism.

As we saw in the last chapter, not all liberals base the claim for state neutrality on moral relativism, the view that moral questions are ultimately irresolvable. Another justification is the pragmatic view, as held by Rawls among others, that whatever the respective value of competing moral positions, people, particularly in modern complex multicultural societies, will always disagree about them and the state should adjust itself to this reality, if only to ensure social stability.

Nevertheless, moral relativism provides an apparently powerful defence for state neutrality, and a challenge to it is important for communitarians, as it is for advocates of animal protection. Here, it might be argued that liberal neutrality, as Nagel (1987) has suggested, exaggerates the degree to which judgements on the validity of competing belief systems are not possible. Thus, Nagel (1987: 232) continues, it may well be possible to dismiss the espousal of a belief 'in terms of errors in their evidence, or identifiable errors in drawing conclusions from it, or in argument, judgement, and so forth' and that whilst 'conflicts of religious faith fail this test . . . most empirical and many moral disagreements do not'. Moreover, there are surely some conceptions of the good – health, bodily integrity, wealth, even liberty – to which everyone might aspire (Waldron, 1989: 74–5) as well as 'conceptions of the good which are manifestly unreasonable' (Arneson, 2000: 71). It would be possible then, at the very least, for a limited non-neutral policy to 'seek to root out weeds while acknowledging that there are many flowers any of which might be favoured' (ibid.).

Despite raising the possibility of judging between different moral beliefs, Nagel (1987: 233) interestingly argues that we cannot make such a judgement on the killing of animals for food, along with abortion and sexual conduct. In these areas, he argues, liberal restraint is still necessary. But why? The purpose of animal ethics is to develop arguments to justify one position over another and it is fair to say that it is very successful in this role. There is little doubt, for instance, that, at the very least, partly at least because of the fact that it is known that animals are sentient, we owe direct duties to them and that inflicting unnecessary suffering on them is wrong.

Thus, the *way* in which animals are killed for food matters. There is a widespread consensus, in the West at least, that it is right to ensure as far as possible that the most humane methods are used for killing animals used for a variety of purposes. We can probably go further than this too. As the material reviewed in chapter 1 revealed, there is strong empirical and argumentative evidence that the moral orthodoxy significantly undervalues the moral status of animals, that many of the ways in which they are currently treated is of dubious moral legitimacy, carried out merely because of the human species' control over animals.

In this context, neutrality and toleration of competing conceptions of the good amounts to 'betraying your own values' (Nagel, 1987: 222). In the words of Goodin and Reeve (1989: 2), neutrality:

> masks vacillation, the absence of intellectual or political courage, an unwillingness to make hard decisions and difficult choices, an abdication of responsibility, and an indifference to the actual fate of the individuals whom it makes a formal claim to flourish.

For Harrison (1979: 285–7), similarly, whilst it is possible from a metaethical perspective to argue that one moral system is as good as another – in terms, for instance, of its internal consistency – no participant in normative ethics with a moral view of his own could make the case for toleration of competing moral positions. 'It is true', Harrison (287) writes:

> that we could understand a man who said, 'All moralities apart from mine are equally good' ... But if he said, 'All moralities including mine are equally good' we should be at a loss. Could, for example, a Christian who admitted that other religious/ moral positions were just as good as Christianity still be regarded as a Christian?

Of course, we can never be certain about the competing value of many conceptions of the good, but, as Arneson (2000: 77) points out 'if one sets the threshold of supporting reasons for public policy at the level of certainty, it is doubtful that any proposed policy can pass'.

A linked argument here is that if we accept the view, as expressed by Barry (1995: 169), that 'no conception of the good can justifiably be held with a degree of certainty that warrants its imposition on those who reject it', then does not the same apply to conceptions of the right? Sandel (1998: 204) is correct here to say that 'modern democratic societies are teeming with disagreements about justice'. Should we not, for instance, then reject the distributive principles recommended by Rawls on the grounds that others, in particular the libertarian approach adopted among others by Nozick (1974), challenge their validity?

One possible difference between questions about the good and the right is that the former tend to be mere prejudices, a product of emotion rather than rationality. As Sher (1997: 144–5) rightly responds, however, arguments about rights or justice 'seem more likely to be swayed both by emotions such as envy, resentment, and fear, and by motives such as selfishness, and solidarity with favoured economic classes'. Another way round this problem is to distinguish between disagreements about principles of justice, on the one hand, and disagreements about how they should be applied on the other (Sandel, 1998: 204). Disagreements of the latter kind, it is suggested, tend to apply to questions of justice – as in agreeing, for instance, about the validity of free speech but not about what should be covered – whereas moral and religious disagreements tend to be of the former kind reflecting 'incompatible conceptions of the good life' (*ibid.*).

It is inaccurate, however, to describe most of the disagreements about justice as being about mere application. The debate between Rawls and Nozick, to take just one example, is about fundamental principles, and many other debates in the sphere of justice are of a similar kind. Sandel (1998: 205–7) interprets Rawls as responding to this by saying that whilst pluralism amongst principles of justice is permitted it must be a 'reasonable pluralism'. Presumably, then, for Rawls, the liberatarian critique of the difference principle is not reasonable and therefore should be rejected. If this is Rawls's position, the problem is obvious. For 'if we can reason about controversial principles of distributive justice ... why can we not reason in the same way about conceptions of the good?' (Sandel, 1998: 207), and decide on balance that some are, after critical reflection, better than others.

A third substantive argument is that even if moral scepticism cannot be successfully challenged it is by no means clear that it leads to neutrality in any case. As Sher (1997: 142) points out, to move from the position of moral scepticism (that we can never know whether any normative proposition is right or wrong) to state neutrality requires a bridging premise, 'that the state *should not* base its decisions on any proposition whose truth cannot be known'. Since such a premise is itself normative we cannot know whether it is true or not.

Further support for a perfectionist state, and against the imposition of moral pluralism, at least in the context of animal protection, is a critique of the view that conceptions of the good are usually partial and may benefit the articulate, wealthy and the powerful in particular. Kymlicka (1989: 900) has suggested that a perfectionist state would:

> serve to distort the free evaluation of ways of life, to rigidify the dominant ways of life, whatever their intrinsic merits, and to unfairly exclude the values and aspirations of marginalized and disadvantaged groups within the community.

Thus, the 'problem of the exclusion of historically marginalised groups is endemic to the communitarian project'. By contrast, 'liberal neutrality has the great advantage of its potential inclusiveness, its denial that subordinated groups must fit into the "way of life" that has been defined by the dominant groups' (Kymlicka, 1990: 227; 228–9).

Leaving aside for a moment the negative impact that so-called liberal 'inclusiveness' has on animals, it should be asked, though, why a perfectionist communitarian state should necessarily fail to include the interests of marginalised groups? The state might play this role. Equally, the state could try to ensure that the advantages available to some privileged groups within civil society are diluted at the state level. Thus, the state might defend the currently dispossessed. And of course, whatever the merits of the neutral state from a human point of view, from the point of view of animals civil society can be a very grim place, one which the only escape may be a perfectionist state putting the protection of animals at the top of its agenda.

A related, and crucial, factor here is that liberal neutrality also exaggerates the degree to which individuals do make unfettered choices. It assumes that individuals choose their plan of life for themselves. Some critics contend, however, that outside influences in moulding an individual's conception of the good life are such that there is little difference between this moulding process and the state itself imposing its preferred conception of the good life (Waldron, 1989: 78). Indeed, it might be preferable for a democratic state to override the sectional influences of civil society.

The application of this critique of liberal neutrality to animals is obvious. As we have intimated, the battle between those with a vested interest in exploiting animals, and those with an interest in protecting them is, in many ways, a battle of ideas. In this sense, conceptions of the good as far as animals are concerned do not exist in isolation of those organisations and individuals seeking to influence others. Indeed, in recent years the animal research and food communities have learnt that they must seek to challenge more effectively the increasingly effective campaigns mounted by the animal protection movement.

Organizations seeking to defend the use of animals in scientific procedures, for instance, now spend as much of their time and, considerable, resources seeking to influence public opinion as they do lobbying politicians and officials. In Britain this role was traditionally performed by the Research Defence Society, founded in 1908, but its perceived failure in the 1980s to get its message across resulted in a much broader-based campaign. In the mid-1980s, the Association of the British Pharmaceutical Industry set up the Animals in Medicines Research Information Centre (AMRIC) which produces glossy information packs, some designed for distribution in school, seeking to justify the use of animals in scientific procedures. Subsequently, AMRIC was joined in the early 1990s by other groups – Seriously Ill for Medical Research and the Research for Health Charities Group – deliberately designed with a campaigning edge to operate in the public arena.

In the agricultural sector, too, industry groups are active in promoting positive images of animals. The battle ground here, as with animal experimentation, is in schools where, in Britain, the NFU competes with animal protection organisations such as the Vegetarian Society to win the hearts and minds of children. Inevitably, industry groups seek to disguise the often grim realities of factory farming. As Mason and Singer (1990: 109) explain, the meat and poultry

CONSERVATISM AND COMMUNITARIANISM 95

industry in America: 'Sponsor colouring books and other materials for children that show farm animals in anthropo- morphic, comic book fantasies. There is no hint, of course, of feed additives, stress, crowding or debeaking.'[2] The meat industry, in addition, has a big advantage over the animal protection movement because of its ability to advertise its products. Positive, and almost universally untrue, images – of happy animals, basking outdoors in bright sunshine, gladly giving themselves on a plate to us – appear on our televi- sion screens nightly. By contrast, because it is regarded as political, animal protection organisations are not allowed a right of reply in the same medium. Given this imbalance of influence, it is nothing short of staggering that up to 10 per cent of Britons describe themselves as vegetarians.

A communitarian case for animals?

Is there, then, a viable communitarian case for the protec- tion of animals? As we saw in the previous chapter, once liberalism is shorn of its pretensions of neutrality, and has to admit a preference for individualism, it is then possible to mount an assault on its key assumptions. Commun- itarians, of course, accuse liberals, in the words of Sher (1997: 12) of 'favouring private, hedonistic, consumption- oriented lives at the expense of solidarity and concern for others'. And, of course, this critique has its resonance in the way animals are treated in liberal societies. Much of the exploitation of animals occurs as a result of consumer demands, for cheaper, and ever-increasing amounts of, food and other products, many of which have to be toxicity tested on animals. The climate created by an individualistic rights- based culture, where animals are denied membership, has also put the survival and well-being of individual humans at the apex of the ruling ideology, irrespective of its impact on animals and nature as a whole.

But what of the communitarian alternative? As Sher (1997: 151–2) has noted, whilst liberal perfectionists tend to be good at telling us *what* the good life should consist in it is not so good at telling us *why* we should prefer liberal values of autonomy and choice and so on. By contrast, communitarians are better at the why rather than telling us what 'our traditions, narratives, and the like require of us. Hence ... it is the *content* of the relevant values that has remained obscure'. Is it possible, then, for animals to be included within a communitarian theory of justice? Well, it might. The liberal conception of the good life can be replaced by a communitarian focus on communal well-being whereby animals are regarded, as part of a shared moral code, a part of the community with interests deserving of protection. Moreover, the communitarian emphasis on par- ticularistic rights and obligations would seem to make sense from the perspective of animal protection. Seeking to impose abstract animal rights on human communities, as animal rights advocates do, will have little effect in societies where animals are not valued. Arguably too, in societies where animals are valued the notion of abstract rights for them becomes redundant anyway.

MacIntyre (1999) hints at the possibility of incorporat- ing the interests of animals within a shared moral code. He seeks to explore the implications for moral philosophy of a recognition of human vulnerability, dependence and animality. MacIntryre decries the 'silliness' of Descartes' view that animals lack sentiency (*ibid.*: 13) and, although he does not think animals are necessarily on a par with humans morally, the degree of moral status will depend upon the species being considered (*ibid.*: 45–6), dolphins, in particular, being recognised for their degree of intelligence and therefore moral worth (*ibid.*: 22–8). More importantly, in distinguishing the communitarian spin in MacIntyre's argument, is his insistence on emphasising how animal like and dependent humans are at least at some periods during their lives and how moral relationships should re- cognize this.

The moral relationships MacIntyre has in mind relate to a network of interdependent relationships in a flourishing community in which obligations are owed from some to whom they may not be reciprocated. 'Those who benefit from that communal flourishing', he writes:

> will include those least capable of independent practical rea- soning, the very young and the very old, the sick, the injured,

and the otherwise disabled, and their individual flourishing will be an important index of the flourishing of the whole community. (*ibid.*: 108–9)

Surprisingly, MacIntyre does not say explicitly, but there seems every reason to think that he wants to, or at least is logically driven to, include animals as members and beneficiaries of this flourishing community.

Despite MacIntyre's efforts, however, there are a number of, potentially fatal, problems with communitarianism's status as an appropriate ideological location for animal protection. In the first place, it presupposes, of course, that a shared moral code includes respect for the interests of animals. There is no particular reason why it should. Indeed, as was pointed out in the previous chapter, the opposite extreme of a perfectionist state which actively promotes the exploitation of animals is possible. MacIntyre, as we have seen, seems to suggest that a virtuous society should incorporate respect for animals but it should be said that, to my knowledge, no other communitarian thinker, with one limited exception, has even mentioned the possibility that they might be so incorporated.[3] A passage from Walzer (1992: 65) is representative of the anthropocentric nature of communitarianism. 'The primary good that we distribute to one another', he writes, 'is membership in some *human* community' (my italics).

Moreover, in at least some communitarian accounts, moral particularity is taken to the logical extreme whereby we are obliged to respect the norms operating in any particular society as valid merely because they are socially situated. Taylor (1984: 184–5) invokes Hegel's support for this by citing his distinction between 'sittlichkeit' – referring to the ethical life embodied in a community – and 'moralitat' – referring to abstract principles as yet unrealized in a community. As Taylor (*ibid.*) remarks approvingly: 'The norms of a society's public life are the content of Sitlichkeit', since it 'presupposes that the living practices are an adequate "statement" of the basic norms'. Not all of those labelled communitarians, however, would accept this social convention view of morality. Sandel (1998: x–xi), in the second edition of his major work, for instance, argues, rightly, that 'the mere fact that certain practices are sanctioned by the traditions of a particular community is not enough to make them just. To make justice the creature of convention is to deprive it of its critical character'.

Sandel is unclear whether his claim is that the social convention view of morality is not the 'true' communitarian position or whether he is using it to illustrate why he himself should not be regarded as a communitarian. His preferred position is a critique of neutral liberalism in which 'principles of justice depend for their justification on the moral worth or intrinsic good of the ends they serve' (*ibid.*). Since this is a perfectionist position but not necessarily a communitarian one, I take it that Sandel does not regard himself, first and foremost, as a communitarian. For our purposes, it should be noted that the consequence for animals of the social convention position is grim, since no community in the world has adopted a norm of moral equality between humans and animals and it is illegitimate to radically criticize this socially embedded norm.

A related argument is that communitarianism, in contrast to other ideologies such as liberalism, eschews the universalism that would ensure that animals are respected everywhere and not just in those communities who decided it was important. Indeed, in this sense, communitarianism would affirm the massive disparities in the treatment of animals that occurs not just in the world but also in the continent of Europe, as indicative of appropriate moral plurality. The idea of being vegetarian on the grounds of morality, for example, is totally foreign in many countries including, for instance, some in Europe and the whole of the Arab world.

We have seen in this chapter, then, that, whilst conservatism and communitarianism offer some glimpses of compatibility with a high level of protection for animals, these are accompanied by severe weaknesses from an animal protection perspective. In particular, the socially-situated emphasis of conservative and communitarian claims, does not sit easily with the necessary focus on universal liberation required by the nature of animal interests, upheld partially in some places and not at all in others. In this sense, liberalism retains a distinct advantage.

Notes

1 The most influential communitarian thinkers have been MacIntyre (1985, 1999), Sandel (1998), Taylor (1979) and Walzer (1983). Etzioni (1999) and Tam (1998) offer more practical analyses of the public policy implications of communitarianism. Useful collections of essays can be found in Etzioni (1995) and Sandel (1984). The debate between liberalism and communitarianism is covered in a book-length study by Mulhall and Swift (1996).

2 Debeaking, or beak trimming, is a controversial procedure first practised in the 1940s which involves the use of a heated blade to cut off about a third of a chick's bill. This practice will be prohibited within the EU from 2010.

3 Etzioni (1995: 21) raises the possibility of animal rights but is non-committal about their validity, implying that they are ruled out because as animals cannot reciprocate they cannot fulfil their obligations to the community.

5

Socialism and animals

In this chapter the relationship between socialist ideology, broadly defined, and the protection of animals is explored. What this exploration reveals is a mixed picture. We find that there is some affinity between the left and animal protection, witnessed by support for animal issues by legislators of left of centre parties, and more general, and largely forgotten, historical links between the two movements. We might speculate that animal protection has been attractive to the left because animals are perceived as another exploited group that needs defending. As we shall see, to provide intellectual ballast to these speculations and empirical evidence, a sustained theoretical attempt to incorporate animals within the socialist pantheon has been provided by the British social theorist Ted Benton. However, this attempt is only partially successful, and seems to offer little more than an anthropocentric animal welfare view. Its limitations are, perhaps, reflected in empirical evidence of a great deal of indifference, and sometimes hostility, on the part of the left about animal issues.

Legislators, the left and animal protection

My own research (Garner, 1999) on the characteristics of those legislators with a particular interest in the issue of animal protection during the 1990s reveals that there was a correlation between support for animal protection and party label. In both Britain and the United States, animal protection was an issue supported predominantly by legislators representing parties of the centre-left. The dominance of the party variable was particularly marked in the United States, where in the five Congresses between 1985–94, the Democrats held 59 per cent of the seats in the House of Representatives but over 80 per cent of those Representatives most committed to animal protection were Democrats.[1] The correlation between party label and action on animal protection is, albeit less obvious, also apparent in Britain. Whereas only 35 per cent of MPs were Labour between 1987–92, 67 per cent of the MPs (24 out of 36) showing the greatest commitment to animal issues were Labour, compared to 22 per cent Conservative (58 per cent in the whole House).

Not only is there a correlation between animal protection advocacy and party label, but the evidence also suggests that support for the issue is particularly prevalent among Labour and Democrat legislators generally considered to be on the left of their respective parties. Thus, of the 24 Labour MPs on the list of the 36 most committed animal protection advocates, no less than 21 (88 per cent) were regarded as either on the 'soft' or 'hard' left of the party and only three – David Clark, Donald Coleman and Alan Williams – were moderates in the centre or on the right of the party. More specifically, seven of the 24 (almost 30 per cent) were associated with the 'hard left' Campaign Group of Labour MPs, which had a total membership of about 40 in the 1987 Labour intake of 229 (17 per cent).[2]

In the United States, where party labels are less important as guides to political action and where there has never been a strong socialist movement, it is significant nevertheless that those Democrats most supportive of animal protection issues tend to represent voting districts in the traditionally more liberal areas of the North East and West. Further confirmation of the correlation between liberal leanings and support for animal protection is provided by an examination of the approval ratings given to members of the House by organisations generally regarded as liberal. For example, 93 (29 per cent) of the 325 members re-elected to the 103rd Congress were given approval ratings of 75 per cent or over by the liberal organisation Americans for Democratic Action (ADA) (U.S. Congress Handbook, 1993: 210–17). By contrast, of the 37 members of the 103rd

Congress (excluding freshmen) who scored highest on animal protection issues, no less than 19 (51 per cent) received approval ratings of 75 per cent or over from ADA.

The Left and the animal protection movement

Further support for ideological compatibility between social-ism and animal protection can be found in the historical links between the labour and socialist movements on the one hand and the animal protection movement on the other. The origins of concern for the welfare of animals, for in-stance, can be located as part of the Victorian social reform movement within which radicals and socialists were active (Ryder, 1989: chapter 7). Most suffragettes, for example, tended also to be in the forefront of campaigns against vivi-section. In a similar vein, William Wilberforce was not only an anti-slavery campaigner but was also a founding member of the RSPCA and Lord Shaftesbury, the author of the Fac-tory Acts and a key figure in the formation of the National Society for the Prevention of Cruelty to Children, was also a campaigner against cruelty to animals. In the United States, likewise, Henry Bergh – the founder of the American Society for the Prevention of Cruelty to Animals – was instrumental in setting up the New York Society for the Prevention of Cruelty to Children and, indeed, the ASPCA prosecuted a child cruelty case by using statutes designed to protect animals (Fisen and Fisen, 1994: chapter 2).

Moreover, as Keane (1998: 132–34) has documented, many activists and leading members of the Independent Labour Party (ILP) and the Social Democratic Federation (SDF) – two of the socialist societies that helped to form what became the Labour Party – endorsed vegetarianism and anti-vivisection. To give one example of cross-cutting sup-port, Keane (*ibid*.: 133) cites the example of Isabella Ford, a Yorkshire socialist who was a member of the ILP, an ardent feminist, anti-vivisectionist and chair of the Leeds branch of the RSPCA. The Fabian Society, the third, and most important, of the socialist societies that created the Labour party, also had links with vegetarianism. As Spencer (1995: 278–9) records, it was members of the National Food Reform

Society, formerly the London branch of the Vegetarian Society, who formed the Fellowship of the New Life in 1883, and then the Fabian Society two years later. 'Both groups', Spencer continues, 'were almost solely vegetarian though it was not, by far, their most significant feature'.

There was also affinity between the Humanitarian League and the labour movement. The Humanitarian League, designed to campaign for benevolence to all sentient life, human and animal, was created by the animal rights pioneer, and socialist, Henry Salt in 1891.[4] Some leading labour movement and socialist figures were active in the Humanitarian League, not least George Bernard Shaw – a long-standing vegetarian, Keir Hardie – the first leader of the Labour Party, Edward Carpenter – socialist intellectual and friend of Salt, and Ramsay MacDonald – the first Labour Prime Minister. In 1896, the Humanitarian League drew up a petition for the labour movement in which it was stated that 'vivisection is cruel and inhuman' . . . and that 'all such experimentation on living animals is opposed to the right feelings and true interests of the working classes' (Keane, 1998: 134–5). Many leading figures in the labour movement – including trade unionists Tom Mann and Will Thorne, and Keir Hardie – added their names to the petition.

Perhaps the most compelling illustration of the link between organised labour, social reform and animal welfare was the so-called 'Old Brown Dog' incident which occurred in London during the early part of the twentieth century (Lansbury, 1985). In 1906, anti-vivisectionists – many of whom were also feminists – persuaded Battersea Council to erect a statue of a dog in memory of all the animals used in London's medical research laboratories in general and one particular brown terrier referred to in anti-vivisection literature which had endured repeated use in the laboratories of University College. The inscription (cited in Keane, 1998: 153) under the statute read:

> In memory of the Brown Terrier Dog Done to Death in the Laboratories of University College in February, 1903, after having endured Vivisection extending over more than Two months and having been handed over from one Vivisector to Another Till Death came to his Release. Also in Memory of the 232 dogs Vivisected at the same place during the year 1902. Men and Women of England, how long shall these Things be?

Pressure was put upon the council to have the statue, situated at the centre of a new, working-class housing estate, removed, but councillors refused. As a result, major disturbances ensued with local people physically defending the statue against attempts by medical students to damage or remove it. Eventually, in 1910, the statue was removed by the council resulting in a protest meeting attended by several thousand people including representatives from various trade unions. Lansbury (1985) concludes from this that working class support for anti-vivisection in Battersea at this time was substantial.

Despite the links between the left and animal protection, the issue was never included in early Labour Party policy programmes and, in any case, for much of the first half of the twentieth century animal protection was a neglected issue in Britain, particularly in mainstream party politics. Despite this, Labour politicians continued to give their support to animal issues. For example, leading Labour figures in the first three decades of the twentieth century – including Philip Snowden, George Lansbury, Arthur Henderson, J. R. Clynes, J. H. Thomas and Will Thorne were all happy to be associated with the British Union for the Abolition of Vivisection (Keane, 1998: 180–1).

It was not until the late 1970s that Labour, for the first time, included animal welfare commitments in its general election manifesto, and not until the 1980s that considerable interest in the issue can be discerned. It is interesting to note that animal protection was most prominent in the Labour Party during the 1980s when the left of the party was in the ascendancy. At a local level, for instance, many Labour-controlled London boroughs adopted so-called 'animal charters' citing the importance of animal protection and what could be done about improving it. Moreover, Labour's general election manifesto in 1983 contained a number of radical proposals not seen in previous or subsequent manifestos. Thus, the party committed itself to creating a standing Royal Commission on animal protection in order to review legislation, to ban all forms of hunting with dogs, the live export trade and 'all extreme livestock systems' (Craig, 1990: 382).

Since then, with the exception of hunting, Labour's support for animal protection issues has been intermittent and moderate, although the role of Labour Governments since 1997 in ending cosmetic testing, banning fur farms and agreeing some fundamental reforms to factory farming within the EU should not be forgotten. The prospect of a hunting ban led the Political Animal Lobby, the lobbying arm of the International Fund for Animal Welfare, to make a £1m donation to Labour, the largest single external donation the party has ever received (*Observer*, 1 September 1996).

Socialist hostility and indifference to animal protection

The ideological affinity between socialism, labourism and animal issues should not be exaggerated. Commitments to improve the treatment of animals have historically been conspicuous by their absence from labour movement programmes, so that Keane (1989: 136) can remark that 'individual support (*for animal protection*) was strong; official endorsement by political organisations was weak'. Thus, the ILP, the SDF, nor the Fabian Society, ever discussed animal issues at conferences or meetings (Keane, 1998: 133). Support for animal issues, even from the left, has traditionally tended to come from middle class intellectuals, Shaw and Carpenter being classic examples. It is true that the vast majority of Labour MPs and activists – although not always the party leadership – have always supported the abolition of hunting (Thomas, 1983). Hunting is, however, unique amongst animal issues for appealing to the traditional class-based politics of Labour, the party's longstanding antipathy being a product of the perception that the practice is the preserve of wealthy rural dwellers. In this case, not only is there a victim but also a class-based perpetrator.

Other animal issues have often been met with indifference, if not outright hostility, by socialists, even of the middle class intellectual variety. At the very least, they have been regarded as an unnecessary distraction from the 'true' purpose of the socialist movement, deemed to be the liberation of human beings. Orwell, to give a classic example, was scathing about vegetarianism, regarding it as a middle class fad that, when, as it often was, linked with socialism damaged the left's chances of appealing to 'ordinary voters'. Thus, he wrote that:

> One sometimes gets the impression that the mere words 'Socialism' and 'Communism' draw towards them with magnetic force every fruit-juice drinker, nudist, sandal-wearer, sex-maniac, Quaker, 'Nature Cure' quack, pacifist, and feminist in England. (quoted in Spencer, 1995: 299)

Henry Hyndman, the Marxist leader of the SDF, similarly commented earlier that: 'I do not want the movement to be a depository of odd cranks: humanitarians, vegetarians, anti-vivisectionists and anti-vaccinationists, arty-crafties and all the rest of them' (quoted in Keane, 1998: 133). William Morris, likewise, was critical of vegetarianism, arguing that it would not improve the lives of the working class. Shaw tells a story about dining with William and Jane Morris, noting their contempt for vegetarianism. To mark what she thought was a 'folly', Jane, on one occasion, gave Shaw a pudding with suet in it, only informing him after he had eaten it (Keane, 1998: 127, 132; Spencer, 1995: 283).

Bringing the story up to date, it is difficult to sustain the view that the contemporary animal protection movement is, in any meaningful sense, left wing, nor that the animal issue draws its support from left wing voters in general. Survey research, principally undertaken in the United States, does reveal that animal advocates do tend to share similar political values to those involved in other 'progressive' causes, such as civil rights, women's rights and the environment (Greanville and Moss, 1985; Sperling, 1988: 99–102; Nibert, 1994: 122). But these 'progressive' causes are not necessarily left-wing. Certainly, the animal protection movement is not working-class, the typical animal advocate being white, female, and middle-class.

It is also the case that animal protection campaigns seem to draw support from across the ideological spectrum. To give one example, the campaign against live exports in Britain which became a major issue in the mid-1990s, appeared to draw as much support from middle-class outposts of Tory Britain – in places like Brightlingsea and Shoreham – where voters with no particular political leanings took the lead – as it did from left-leaning activists. As Benton and Redfearn (1996: 51) note, despite the fact that the campaign

was widened even further by the police decision to invoke
the Public Order Act to try to stop the protests, so that
the protests arguably became as much about civil rights and
police powers as it was about animals, the left was conspicuous by its absence. In general terms, as Mills and Williams
(1986) have pointed out: 'Animals, it seems, have not found
a place among the political subjects that the Left considers
important.'

A socialist case for animal protection?

The political sociology of links between the Left and animal
protection cannot by itself, of course, determine our answer
to the theoretical question of compatibility. Having said
that, some of the socialist distrust of vegetarianism and
other animal issues reported above finds its echo in the
anthropocentrism of much socialist thought. Although alternative interpretations of the animal/human relationship
can be derived from the large body of Marx's work (see Noske,
1989: 70–3), much of Marx's thought tends to be irredeemably anthropocentric. This conclusion is reached because
Marx argued, mainly in the *Economic and Philosophical
Manuscripts*, originally published in 1844, that humans have
the capacity for self-reflection and therefore have a 'species
being'. Thus: 'Conscious life activity distinguishes man
immediately from animal life activity. It is just because of
this that he is a species being'. Man 'proves himself a conscious species being' by 'creating a world of objects by his
practical activity, in his work upon inorganic nature' (Clarke
and Linzey, 1990: 43).

Marx admits that animals produce too but 'an animal
only produces what it immediately needs for itself or its
young. It produces one-sidedly, whilst man produces universally' (*ibid.*). Humans, in other words, have the capacity
to transform nature. From this, Marx saw the natural world
primarily as a place to be subjugated and exploited for
human use, with animals described as 'products of nature'.
Through his production, therefore, 'nature appears as his
work and his reality'. In *Capital Vol. 1*, Marx is even more
brutally clear. Nature is to be dominated by humans whose

ability to do so imaginatively makes them what they are. Animals can be regarded as mere 'instruments of labour, along with specially prepared stones, wood bones and shells' (quoted in Mills and Williams, 1986: 30). As Noske (1989: 73) points out:

> Socialism (or communism), the ideal that Marxist's pursue, will be a state where humanity's unity with nature has been fully realized, where nature has been brought to full productivity. One cannot escape the notion that this is taking anthropocentrism to its very extreme.

We need not regard this interpretation of Marx as the last word on the compatibility of socialism and animal protection. An alternative view is represented by the comment by Mills and Williams (1986: 31) that, 'no social formation has been so deeply implicated in the maintenance and proliferation of the mistreatment of animals as capitalism'. So, despite the hostile version of Marx cited above, it can be suggested that animal protection might be regarded as a left-wing issue in the sense that animals are perceived to be another exploited group who are deemed worthy of support by legislators generally concerned with ameliorating the plight of the downtrodden and dispossessed. Moreover, it may also be significant that the modern animal rights movement tends to focus, not on individual acts of cruelty, but on the institutional exploitation of animals in farming and scientific research. Thus, modern intensive animal agriculture is described as 'factory' farming, making an obvious link with human exploitation in the labour market, and laboratories are portrayed as prisons with equally compelling human connotations.[3]

The major adversaries of the animal rights movement are large agribusiness and pharmaceutical corporations, and, although the animal rights movement is not necessarily anti-capitalist or anti-business, there are affinities between its opposition to profit at all costs and the Left's traditional socialist agenda. To give one example, the competitive market in pharmaceuticals leads to the development of so-called 'me-too' drugs, requiring a duplication of animal research because of the need for companies to maintain market secrecy (Sharpe, 1988: 129–30). A great deal of animal suffering could be eliminated if new medical products be restricted to areas of real need where similar formulations were not already available, and this is more likely to occur, of course, in a socialised economy. Moreover, as Noske (1989: 14) points out, there are 'striking parallels' between human industrial workers and the position of animals in factory farms.

We should not exaggerate the links between animal protection and the left's critique of capitalism. If the intention of revealing similarities of treatment is to persuade industrial workers to ally themselves with animals, it will almost certainly end in failure, as indeed it has to date. Moreover, whilst there is something in the claim that competitive capitalist economies intensify the infliction of animal suffering, they can hardly be accused of causing it. Indeed, a future socialist society would, all things being equal, not require cheap factory-farmed food or new safe drugs any less than a capitalist one.

Benton, socialism and animals

At a theoretical level, there has been an attempt, associated with Ted Benton, to rescue socialism, and more specifically Marxism, for animals (see Benton, 1993, 1993a, 1996). Benton adopts a theory of distributive justice based on what he describes as the socialist principle of need, which, for him, should replace rights as the most effective means whereby the interests of animals can be furthered. This facilitates the extension of the boundaries of justice beyond humans, since animals quite clearly have needs that can be satisfied or neglected. Indeed, as Benton (1993: 212) points out, the principle of need allows us to include more species than, say, Regan's subject-of-a-life criterion, and indeed raises the possibility that the community of justice might include non-sentient but living parts of nature as well (see chapter 6). A theory of distributive justice based on need would, for Benton, transform human/animal relationships. It would, for instance, rule out factory farming, which deprives animals of meeting most, if not all, of their needs (see below).

Benton draws upon Marxists' traditional suspicion of rights to suggest that liberal rights language may not be the most appropriate way of protecting animals (see Lukes, 1985). In the first place, the granting of rights is arguably not the best way of identifying responsibility for wrongdoing in the setting of institutional exploitation. Rights are individualistic in the sense that they assume the existence of an agent who can be held responsible. For a case of cruelty to companion animals, or, in some circumstances, wild animals, this model is usually appropriate because it is possible to identify a distinct transgressor. Such a model is not really appropriate, on the other hand, for the institutional exploitation of animals which occurs mainly in factory farms and laboratories, since in such a setting the issue of ownership is confused. In such an environment, it is difficult to identify who is responsible for the infringement of rights. Benton (1993: 89–90) sets out the problem thus:

> Should we assign responsibility to the operatives who administer and maintain the animals and the physical plant, to their managers, or to the business executives who run the enterprise, or to the investors in the pension schemes who supply its capital, or to the food processors and retailers who demand standardized and predictable supplies of meat at set prices, or to consumers who demand cheap food and ask no questions, or to legislators who fail to outlaw these practices, to a civil service which fails to enforce what legislation there is, or to a citizenry that fails to act against abuse?

The obvious answer here is to say that we should assign responsibility to *all* of them. But then are they all equally culpable or should we assign primary responsibility to a particular group?

Secondly, following another familiar Marxist theme, since the 'requirement for rights is . . . only a symptom of social pathology and moral disintegration', it is far better to effect a transformation of society where the need for rights is either eradicated or at least reduced (Benton, 1996: 35). Even for humans, there is a world of difference between proclaiming the existence of rights and upholding them in practice. So, despite the fact that governments throughout the world proclaim human rights, this has not ensured that human exploitation and suffering has been eliminated. This is not surprising given the context of the vastly unequal nature of modern capitalist societies where 'for the majority, rights are merely abstract, formal entitlements with little or no *de facto* purchase on the realities of social life' (Benton, 1993a: 166). If individuals are to gain the benefits that rights are designed to produce, therefore, it is necessary to ensure that the, primarily material, conditions are right.

The parallel with animals is obvious. As Benton suggests (1996: 40), 'more benign and compassionate moral sentiments' towards them are likely to come about only when they are ceased to be regarded as expendable commodities in an industrialized and mechanized system of exploitation. In other words, reflecting the traditional Marxist distinction between the formal possession of rights and their substantive enjoyment, there is little point in according rights to animals unless there is a substantial change in attitudes towards them. For Benton (1993: 94), then:

> rights are unlikely to be effective in practice unless those who have the power to abuse them are already benevolently disposed to their bearers ... Where humans gain their livelihood from a practice which presupposes a 'reification' of animals, or gain pleasure from sports which involve systematic animal suffering, it seems unlikely that a rational argument that this treatment is unjust to the animals concerned would be sufficient to make the humans concerned change their ways.

It would seem to follow that a change in their ways can only be produced by a radical shift in social relations. What is required, then, is a change in social attitudes towards both humans and animals to ensure that the aim of according rights – to ensure that the recipients are treated with respect and as ends-in-themselves – is achieved.

So, although Benton, as one would expect from a Marxist, does think that nonhuman animals can suffer through the exercise of human property rights (1996: 166), the implication of his view is that the property status of animals will only be abolished when social attitudes have changed, and the benefits that come to individuals from being rights bearers will, likewise, only be felt when those with the opportunity to infringe them are no longer disposed to do so. The debate around legal status, then, becomes of secondary importance since it is merely a reflection of wider societal attitudes. Moreover, because the formal granting of

rights and legal status to humans and animals are secondary
to societal attitudes, the need to formally accord rights, of
freedom or anything else, becomes redundant once societal
attitudes change. In other words, the imposition of formal
rights is predicated on the existence of a competitive individualism whereby humans need protecting against each
other, and animals need protecting against humans. Remove
the cause of this conflict and it is possible to remove the need
for formal legalistic notions of rights.

An assessment

Benton's attempt to apply Marxism to animals is only
partially successful. He is right to argue that a socialist
principle of distributive justice, based on needs rather than
deserts, presents 'no ontological obstacle to its extension
beyond species boundaries' (Benton, 1993: 212). If we consider Marx's own formulations (1969: 159–60) it is very clear
that his preferred distributive principle – or at least the one
he thought would emerge in a communist society – 'from
each according to his ability to each according to his needs'
– is able to incorporate animals whereas his interpretation
of the desert principle, 'the individual ... receives back
from society ... exactly what he gives to it', is difficult to
apply to them. Benton is also correct to say that according
rights to animals is of limited usefulness in the context of
institutional exploitation.

Two initial weaknesses of Benton's position are worth
stating at this point. In the first place, Benton's socialist
theory of needs, whilst entirely plausible, is not the only
theory of justice that can incorporate animals. Benton is
right to suggest that it is difficult to see how a theory of
justice based on desert could apply to animals. However,
we could conceivably base our incorporation of animals on
the entitlement principle, or on the utility principle, or
indeed, the Rawlsian principle that goods should be distributed to benefit the least advantaged (Dobson, 1998: 63).
We need not, therefore, adopt a socialist theory of needs
to incorporate the interests of animals within a theory of
justice.

More significantly, secondly, Benton's theory of need seems to lead to a commitment to a significant difference in the moral worth of humans and animals and, as such, his conclusions will not satisfy those who are persuaded of the case for the moral objectionability of meat eating and animal experimentation. He seems clear that if animal needs are to be satisfied then radical changes to the present relationship between humans and animals is required, although this will vary radically from one species to another (Benton, 1993: 212–13). Thus, on animal agriculture, he points out that 'If animal husbandry is tolerable at all' then those 'husbandary regimes which preserve opportunities for animals to establish and maintain the broad patterns of social life which are peculiar to their species' are to be preferred (Benton, 1993: 172). This would rule out factory farming because it imposes:

> massive constraints and distortions on the mode of life of species of non-human animals caught up in them. Their lives are sustained solely to serve purposes external to them, conditions and exercise of their species-power are denied to them, and, more specifically, their social needs and capacities are systematically denied and suppressed. (Benton, 1993: 59)

Benton is right to argue that the needs of humans and animals, and indeed the needs of different species of animals, will differ. Most pro-animal philosophers would not dissent from this. It does not make sense, for instance, to provide for animals a right to vote. However, the conclusion they would draw from the equal consideration of interests principle, as Singer and others have called it, is that where human and animal interests coincide, as they do, it is argued, in the case of the avoidance of pain, then there is no reason to treat a human ability to experience pain as somehow more worthy of being relieved. In other words, if rights theory is utilized, this would amount to saying that an animal has a right not to have pain inflicted on it for the benefit of humans and/or other animals.

The equal consideration of needs or interest principle, therefore, rather begs the question as to what needs or interests humans and animals have. We might want to say, for instance, that animals have very few needs, if any, and humans have many complex needs. For the pro-animal

philosophers, animals, or at least some of them, have considerable needs, most of which are not being met by cur-
rent practices. Indeed, for some pro-animal philosophers,
animals have an interest in staying alive which ought to
be taken into account in our moral deliberations. Benton
does not, however, seem to share the view that human and
animal needs are remotely similar. As he writes (1993: 214–
15):

> The complexity and multi-dimensionality of need in the hu-
> man case renders humans vulnerable to a range of sources and
> types of harm to which individuals of other species are onto-
> logically insusceptible ... Any conception of justice adequate
> to cross-species encounters would be required to be sensitive
> to such differences in the structure and scope of need, and would
> license appropriate differences of treatment.

We are getting closer now to a real understanding of
Benton's position. He identifies two different principles of
justice, what he calls a 'difference-respecting egalitarian
principle of justice' (the type associated with pro-animal
philosophers such as Singer), on the one hand, and a 'perfectionist' view (which grounds differences of entitlement
in possession of different attributes, or 'excellences'), on the
other. But when Benton asks rhetorically (1993: 215) if we
can 'sustain' the distinction between these two principles
he answers in the negative. The former concertinas into
the latter. As a result, the 'licensing of differences of treatment amounts to the abandonment of an egalitarian view
of justice'.

Benton seems to be saying here, then, that animals are
morally inferior to humans and, presumably, the interests
of the former can be sacrificed to uphold at least some
interests of the latter. And sure enough he goes on to say
that: 'In the face of continuing human/animal conflicts of
need, grounds can be provided ... for meeting the needs of
humans where they necessarily arise at the expense of the
needs of other animals', although, 'what may be justified as
necessary to the meeting of need may not be justified for
just any desire, however trivial or whimsical' (1993: 215).
There has rarely been such an eloquent statement of the
anthropocentric moral orthodoxy, the animal welfare view
that only the infliction of suffering on animals which serves

no significant human need or interest should be prohibited. Have we come so far for so little? The application of a socialist theory of need to animals ends up justifying pretty much the status quo. This is hardly a position that should make a socialist comfortable!

Benton's most interesting contribution to the animals debate is not his, deeply disappointing, argument relating to what we should be permitted to do to animals, but the case he puts forward for a Marxist political praxis for the animal protection movement. Here, Benton (1993: 93) is right to point out that there is a crucial difference between the animal liberation movement and other human liberation movements in the sense that the latter:

> are able themselves to articulate and press the claims which constitute their moral rights. In the case of animals there is a necessary and permanent incapacity to recognize and articulate their own moral status as rights-holders. The rights of animals must always be claims made on behalf of, and never by, animals themselves.

Benton suggests that not only does this provide a strategic problem for the animal protection movement but that it also reduces the force of animal protection claims, presumably because: 'There is an inescapable moment of paternalism in the attribution of rights to non-human animals' (1993: 93), and therefore we cannot be sure that this is want animals really want.

Benton is right when he says that the inability of animals to articulate their own case for liberation is hugely problematic strategically. Although he does not argue this point explicitly, the possibility of associating the liberation of animals with other dispossessed groups – for socialists the economically poor – would, if successful, offer a way forward not available in liberalism. There is, I think, less of a case for saying that the inability of animals to liberate themselves diminishes the normative case for animal liberation. After all, as Benton (1993: 93–4) himself admits, some oppressed human groups, such as slaves, had to have their case largely articulated by other humans, and campaigns for young children and the mentally disabled are similarly paternalistic in character. Of course, if we do not know what the needs of animals are then we will be unable to articulate them correctly. But surely this is not an insuperable obstacle. After all, we know a great deal about animal behaviour now and are likely to know more in the future.

Benton correctly observes that, although abolishing the property status of animals is a necessary step towards the liberation of animals, it is not a sufficient step without a fundamental transformation of the way in which animals are regarded. As we argued in chapter 2, this analysis has a great deal of validity. It is worth repeating Benton's relevant assertion here that (1993: 94) 'rights are unlikely to be effective in practice unless those who have the power to abuse them are already benevolently disposed to their bearers'. The question here is how this transformation is to be effected. For a liberal animals advocate, in the absence of a movement for self-liberation, this is to be achieved through persuading others that the arguments culminating in the granting of rights to animals are eminently plausible, thereby making institutional exploitation illegitimate.

For Benton the emphasis on the realm of ideas will never do. Rather, change will only be effected when it coincides with social and economic change, coupled with the existence of a liberationary class. Now, it is plausible to suggest that relationships between humans can be altered positively through social, and particularly economic, reform that removes or reduces the need for competitiveness and exploitation. Indeed, Marx is justly credited with emphasising the impact of economic factors on human behaviour. Applying this approach to animals, however, is likely to be much less successful. It would seem to mean that in order for animals to be regarded in a more positive light the abolition of institutional exploitation is required. But how is this to be achieved, particularly since animals are not capable of their own liberation, and the liberal method of persuasion is not open to us? To be taken more seriously as candidates for ideological preference as far as animal protection is concerned, then, Green Marxists have to show us how this circular argument is to be broken. Otherwise, it would seem premature, at the very least, to dispense with rights discourse.

We have seen in this chapter that there have been attempts to link socialism with animal protection, both theoretically and in practice. It is not clear, however, that the irredeemably anthropocentric nature of much socialist thought can be rescued for animal advocates. Benton provides the most sophisticated attempt to date but its success in emphasising needs and recognizing the social, economic and political context of rights needs to be set against the acceptance of an anthropocentric ethic and the failure to offer an alternative viable agency for the protection of animals. The fact that interest in animal issues by the left in practice has been rather intermittent and superficial is indicative of the human-centred goal of the socialist project. On this score, it might be more profitable to consider what a non-anthropocentric ethic has to offer for the protection of animal interests. It is to this possibility we turn in the next chapter.

Notes

1 Details of the research, including the scoring system adopted to arrive at the names of those legislators in Britain and the United States with the best records on animal protection, can be found in my article (1999).

2 This information was gleaned from Roth (1988).

3 See Spiegel (1988), which explicitly makes the link between human and animal oppression.

4 Ryder (1989: 127) points out that 'Salt was a prolific author, although never a best-seller. Of some forty-six titles including revisions, four were poetry, two advocated vegetarianism, one was about socialism, two were classical, two were on wild flowers, six were on Shelley and ten were to do with the rights of animals.' His best-known work on animal rights was Salt (1980), originally published in 1892.

6

Ecology and animals

Superficially, it might be supposed that there is a good fit between the protection of animal interests and environmentalism since it is the one ideology considered in this book that focuses on the nonhuman realm. As this chapter will reveal, however, the fit is not as close as might be supposed. In the first place, much of what passes for environmentalism, at least in the practical sense, is anthropocentric in nature, condemning animals to be the servants of human interests. Secondly, even though the strand of environmentalism often described as ecologism (Dobson, 2000: 1–4) does remove humans from the moral pedestal, thereby setting it apart from traditional Western schools of thought, its holistic nature, and its inclusion of the whole of nature within the moral realm, generates severe conflicts with the protection of individual animals. Attempts to reconcile environmental ethics with animal rights/liberation views have, so far at least, failed to bridge the gap.

Anthropocentric environmentalism

A great deal of environmental thought and practice is human-centred in the sense that the main purpose of protecting the natural world is for human benefit (Passmore, 1974). These benefits are often economic, but may also be medicinal, cultural, or aesthetic. Anthropocentric environmentalism, then, regards the value of the natural world, including animals, as extrinsic to its use for humans. It is therefore equivalent to the indirect duty view we came across in chapter 1. According to this view, animals have no intrinsic value, and their protection is totally dependent on whether it serves human interests to do so. It is not even equivalent, in terms of the moral worth accorded to animals, to the animal welfare position which, even though it accords an inferior moral status to animals, does at least postulate some moral worth or standing to them.

Virtually all international wildlife treaties emphasize the benefits to humans of conservation. Some, such as the Convention for the Protection of Birds Useful to Agriculture – signed in 1902 – and the International Convention for the Regulation of Whaling – signed in 1946 (on which see below) – were set up explicitly to protect economic interests. Similarly, a treaty to protect birds, signed by the United States and Japan in 1972, refers to their 'aesthetic' qualities whilst the preamble to a bilateral treaty concluded by the United States and the Soviet Union in 1976 states that 'migratory birds are a natural source of great scientific, economic, aesthetic, cultural educational, and recreational ... value'. Two of the major wildlife treaties echo similar sentiments. The Convention on Wetlands of International Importance Especially as Waterfowl Habitat (better known as the Ramsar treaty) explains that wetlands 'constitute a resource of great economic, cultural, scientific and recreational value', whilst the Convention on the Conservation of Migratory Species of Wild Animals (the Bonn Convention) emphasises that 'wild animals ... must be conserved for the good of mankind' (Lyster, 1985: 75–6, 180).

This anthropocentric emphasis explains why there is a preoccupation with endangered species in national and international wildlife conservation, since human losses (economic, medicinal, aesthetic) are likely to follow from the disappearance of an extinct species but not from the loss of individual animals where this does not threaten the species as a whole. Thus, the 'central focus of world conservation politics' is the CITES treaty (Convention on International Trade in Endangered Species) which came into force in 1975 (Boardman, 1981: 94) and has now been adopted by 130 countries. The aim of the treaty is to restrict trade in some species and prohibit trade in other (more endangered) species. It is not the purpose of the treaty to explicitly prohibit killing or the infliction of suffering on endangered animals, but the treaty does seek to remove one of the major causes of, and justifications for, the killing of members of endangered species (Lyster, 1985: 91).

This anthropocentrism explains too why the protection of wild animals has at least as high a public profile as any animal issue. Public policy outputs designed to conserve wildlife have been extensive and sometimes stringent. Similarly, the wildlife protection groups – such as the Royal Society for the Protection of Birds and the World Wide Fund for Nature – have larger memberships and bigger incomes than the 'pure' animal protection organisations which tend to focus on domesticated animals in farms and laboratories (Garner, 1998: chapter 4). It is not difficult to see why this is the case. Protecting wildlife not only appeals to those who regard animals as having intrinsic value, but also, crucially, appeals to those who recognize the variety of human interests served by protecting it.

Anthropocentrism in action

The classic example of an anthropocentric wildlife treaty is the International Convention for the Regulation of Whaling, originally created in 1946. This treaty, under which there is now a moratorium on commercial whaling, was designed to conserve the animals, not because they were regarded as intrinsically valuable and therefore worthy of some respect and decent treatment, but because whaling nations recognized that they needed to be conserved in order for hunting them to continue. The convention set up a standing body, the International Whaling Commission (IWC), which is designed to regulate the industry by imposing annual quotas determined by calculating the maximum sustainable yield. In 1982, the IWC decided that stocks were at a sufficiently low level to introduce a moratorium (in 1986) on commercial whaling and this remains to the present day.

The whaling treaty was therefore, at least as originally conceived, irredeemably anthropocentric. The implication was that as soon as whale stocks recovered, the moratorium would cease and quotas reinstated. The fact that this has so far failed to happen, despite much lobbying from whaling nations such as Japan and Norway, reveals an interesting clash in values which throws light on the ethics of wildlife conservation. The moratorium remains partly because there is uncertainty over numbers, but, now that non-whaling nations predominate on the IWC, other values have taken centre-stage. To some extent no doubt, public opposition to whaling, in Britain, America and elsewhere, is based on the feeling that whales have intrinsic value and it is therefore against their interests to suffer and be killed. Equally, other anthropocentric values – and in particular the view that whales are majestic creatures and on aesthetic grounds should be protected – have emerged to challenge the economic and cultural interests of whaling nations.

Insofar as anthropocentric reasons for protecting whales are used, it should be asked if they have any right to be regarded as superior to the equally anthropocentric justifications used in defence of exploiting them. This is particularly the case as opposition to whaling comes from countries, such as Britain, where animals are exploited, in factory farms and laboratories, with ruthless efficiency. Is not this a case of the copper calling the kettle black? Indeed, arguably whaling is not as bad morally as the treatment of domesticated animals. As Scully (2002: 289) points out:

> The sole difference – that in the one case we are dealing with wild animals, and in the other with animals born and bred just for our use – actually works to the favour of the killers. Their prey at least enjoyed some modicum of freedom. Their victims, at least, were not subjected to lives of unremitting pain and privation. And they, at least, were willing to do the job themselves.

A related conflict in the politics of international wildlife conservation concerns the debate surrounding so-called 'sustainable use'. This has particularly centred on African game and most notably the elephant. The elephant population's decline, precipitated by the market value of ivory, led to its inclusion on the CITES list of species in which trade is prohibited. In some countries, most notably Kenya, elephants and rhinos have been zealously protected with wardens in some national parks given the power to kill poachers. This kind of blanket protection is enormously controversial because of the danger, and sometimes reality, that it takes place at the expense of local indigenous populations who are deprived of land and the opportunity to exploit the protected animals.

It is in this context that the debate about sustainable use has arisen. Arguing that elephant populations have recovered sufficiently, a number of Southern African countries – led by South Africa, Zimbabwe and Botswana – have, for some time, practiced a policy of sustainable use. This involves culling a regulated number of elephants each year and distributing the benefits (in terms of the proceeds from meat, hides, ivory, and in some cases from allowing tourists to kill game) amongst the local communities, the best known scheme being the Communal Areas Management Programme for Indigenous Resources (CAMPFIRE) in Zimbabwe (see *Guardian*, 20 May 1997). The problem is that this strategy requires, above all, the reopening of the ivory trade in order that the market price increases. When the elephant was added to Appendix I, the states who practised this strategy exempted themselves and they are now campaigning for a resumption of the trade on a larger scale.

The reopening of the ivory trade is argued for on the grounds that this is not only a good conservation strategy – because it provides an incentive for indigenous populations to protect the animals because they will benefit financially from it – but also because, by confirming the moral superiority of humans over animals – however endangered they may be – it is just. The pressure to adopt a sustainable use strategy has been immense, and the sustainable use campaigners have had some success with CITES permitting a limited resumption of the ivory trade. In 1997, the parties to the CITES treaty agreed to the transfer of elephants from Appendix 1 (of endangered species), to Appendix 2 (of threatened species) of the CITES treaty. This then allowed Namibia, Botswana and Zimbabwe to resume, in a very limited fashion, marketing ivory. Only a relatively small amount of existing stockpiles can be sold, Japan is to be the sole trading partner and mechanisms must be in place to counter the emergence of a black market. Another similar limited sale was agreed in 2002 (*Guardian*, 13 November 2002).

Superficially, this conflict over sustainable use may seem like a battle of ideas, between those who think that animals should be a resource for us, and those who seek to protect them even when this may harm the interests of some humans. In reality, the picture is rather less clear than this. Generally, conservation organisations and most governments in developed countries have been opposed to sustainable use. For some, the motives behind this may well involve a consideration that it is wrong to cull animals because they have interests in not suffering and being killed. There is more than a sneaking suspicion, though, that the opposition to sustainable use is motivated by equally blatant anthropocentric motives. It is easy for Western governments and peoples to advocate and support the protection of animals when they themselves do not benefit from their exploitation. Indeed, Western governments have everything to lose in terms of public opinion by considering the economic case for, say, whaling or the ivory trade. Furthermore, this public opinion is also arguably motivated mainly by anthropocentric values, since concern for wild animals tends to focus on those attractive animals – such as the elephant, the polar bear, the whale and nonhuman primates – whose extinction would be regarded as a greater loss (primarily, presumably, for aesthetic reasons) than the disappearance of a less attractive species.

The result of this excessive anthropocentric attention devoted to endangered wild animals is a clear case of double standards which amounts to a kind of 'eco-imperialism'. For what often exists in modern wildlife conservation is not so much a conflict between the interests of animals and humans. Rather, it is a conflict between competing *human* interests. Those (such as whalers and developing world governments and peoples) who stand to gain from the exploitation of endangered species (and, indeed, other species of wild animals to whom the developed nations attach some importance) and who stand to lose by allowing the protection of such animals to come before development projects which have enormous human benefits, are expected to sacrifice their interests whilst the developed world continues to exploit animals by the millions in factory farms and laboratories.

Explaining the ethical positions underlying wildlife conservation is one thing, justifying one particular course of action is quite another. The implication of the arguments in the preceding paragraph is that the adoption of an anthropocentric ethic makes it much more difficult to justify the protection of wild animals, even if they are members of an endangered species. From an anthropocentric perspective, therefore, the case for a sustainable use approach is well nigh unanswerable. Only an animal rights ethic can offer the comprehensive protection for wild animals that Western public opinion seems to want. There are two caveats though that may seem less attractive to such an audience, although not to the present author. First, an animal rights ethic offers protection for all wild animals and not just those species that are regarded as the most attractive. Secondly, consistency and justice demands that an animal rights ethic is applied to all animals and not just wild animals. The consequence of this, of course, is that farm and laboratory animals would be protected too and, indeed, the use of animals for such practices may well be rendered illegitimate morally.

Ecocentrism and animal rights

In contrast to an anthropocentric justification for protecting wild animals and nature, the ecocentric position, often referred to as an environmental ethic,[1] is concerned with recognizing the intrinsic vale of nonhumans. This position – often referred to as 'deep ecology' – holds that nonhuman elements of nature have an intrinsic value, independently of their use value for humans. An ecocentric ethic, then, holds that nonhuman animals have moral standing, that they can be morally harmed directly, and what we do to them should not merely be judged by the benefits to humans of a particular course of action. Ecocentrism would seem, then, to represent a particularly fertile ground for animal advocates. Not only does it accord moral standing to animals, but it also offers the possibility, unlike animal welfare, of greater moral equality between humans and the other animals.

However, despite the apparent fit, there are also doubts about its appropriateness as an ideal location for the protection of animals. In the first place, moral standing for deep ecologists is extended beyond sentient beings to encompass living, but not sentient, parts of nature as well as inanimate objects such as mountains and deserts. Such a project, of course, has to dispense with mental complexity and sentiency as the benchmark for moral standing, a criterion adopted by the vast majority of animal rights/liberationists.

Attempts to justify according moral worth to non-sentient and inanimate objects are, to say the least, problematic, and is denied by most animal rights/liberation thinkers. For them, the moral standing of sentient beings is based on their capacity to suffer, so that it would seem to make sense to say that we can not only harm a sentient being but also wrong him or her. It is less clear how we can wrong a non-sentient being (Frey, 1983: 154–5). Earlier, we saw Singer (1981: 123) point out that: 'There is genuine difficulty in understanding how chopping down a tree can matter *to the tree* if the tree can feel nothing.' The possession of interests, then, for most animal rights/liberation thinkers, presupposes desires, which can be promoted or thwarted by the actions of others, and the capacity to desire presupposes consciousness or sentiency.

An alternative, middle-way, 'biocentric' position is to assign moral worth to living parts of nature, thereby including more than those who are sentient but excluding the inanimate objects accorded moral worth by ecocentrics (Taylor, 1986). Whilst this may be a more satisfactory moral position, it still does not, of course, help us to restore sentiency to the centre of moral reasoning. Using life, as opposed to sentiency, as the benchmark for moral standing allows us to suggest that living things can be characterised by the property of 'autopoiesis' which refers to self-production or self-renewal. As a result, it is argued, living things can have interests and a good of their own – benefiting from environments in which they can reproduce and repair themselves – even though they are not aware of it (Eckersley, 1992: 60–1). The problem here though is it remains unclear how this enables us to distinguish morally between living things and inanimate objects, both categories of entities having a good which can be harmed, although in the latter case the good is not a biological one (Hayward, 1995: 67).

Ecocentrics, as we have seen, do want to accord moral standing to inanimate parts of nature, and numerous attempts have been made to justify this position (Dobson, 2000: 36–51). One well known approach is to adopt an ecological consciousness based on a 'state of being' (Dobson, 2000: 46–51), a psychological approach urging greater recognition of our connection with nature, so that we come to appreciate, identify and be enriched by it, and in turn want to protect it as if it was ourselves (Fox, 1985; Rodman, 1983; Matthews, 1991). Because this would seem to amount to saying that 'if I am part of nature, it is in my interests to try and protect it', it has been suggested that the 'state of being' approach is in reality anthropocentric (Hayward, 1995: 71). As such, it is open to the objection that our ethical judgement whether or not to protect nature becomes contingent on humans becoming connected to nature. Some, of course, might, but others will not. This also raises the crucial question about how people are to be persuaded to adopt this environmental 'state of being'. As Dobson (2000: 50) remarks, if, as one ecologist has suggested:

> 'Deep ecology ... requires openness to the black bear, becoming truly intimate with the black bear, so that honey dribbles down your fur coat as you catch the bus to work' ... then deep ecology would seem to be in deep trouble. The guffaws that generally greet this kind of statement reveal deep ecology's profound problem of persuasion.

And this brings us back to the relationship between deep ecology and the protection of nonhuman animals. For the key point to make is that if we adopt an ecocentric ethic, we are obliged to accept the case for extending moral worth to the whole of nature, or at least to living things. As has been indicated, one problem with this is that it is politically much harder to sustain than building the moral standing of animals on sentiency or mental complexity. Even more importantly, however, an ecocentric ethic lies on intellectually shaky foundations.

Holism in ecological thought

An additional, and more important, incompatibility between an ecocentric ethic and a viable ethic for the protection of animals is the tendency in Green thinking, of ecocentric and anthropocentric hues, to emphasize the importance of whole ecosystems or species or the concept of diversity itself, rather than the individuals within ecosystems or species. As we saw above, this emphasis may be designed to serve human ends, but equally, it may be justified on the non-anthropocentric grounds that the extinction of a species can alter the balance of an ecosystem, thereby damaging the interests of all of its members. This non-anthropocentric position held, amongst others, by biocentric thinkers such as Taylor (1986) does not, as Attfield (2003: 10) points out, 'deny that ecosystems have great value' but that 'this value arises . . . from the way that ecosystems facilitate the lives and the flourishing of the numerous individual creatures that comprise them or depend on them'. A more recent statement of this kind of ecological holism came from Robert Goodin (1992: 1–2) whose statement, in an article for the initial edition of the journal *Environmental Politics* is worth quoting at length:

> Rather than worrying about localised forest fires burning individual bears, environmentalists now tend to worry about the destruction of whole forests and entire ecosystems. Instead of fixating upon individual animals, we now worry about whole species . . . Green causes seem to me somehow more compelling in those newer manifestations. The arguments of animal liberationists notwithstanding, I, for one, have remained at least a half-hearted carnivore; I wear leather shoes; I did not dissuade my aged mother from buying a fur coat. I commit all those sins against the sterner forms of the ecological creed only vaguely apologetically. At the end of the day, I simply do not think that caring about animals one-by-one is what the environmentalist movement is – or ought to be – most centrally all about.

There is a very different non-anthropocentric position. This justifies protecting entities such as ecosystems, or species, or diversity on the grounds that they themselves have moral value and thereby should be protected *whatever the cost* to individuals. Leopold (1949: 217), the father of deep ecology, offered the classic statement of this latter version of what Attfield (2003: 8) has described as 'holistic value theory' when he wrote that 'a thing is right when it tends to preserve the integrity, stability and beauty of the biotic community. It is wrong when it tends otherwise.' In other words, thinkers such as Leopold 'maintain that ecosystems

have a good independent of that of their component individuals, and as such have their own moral standing' (Attfield,
2003: 11).

Holistic value theory is clearly at odds with the individualistic rights or liberation approach to animal ethics.
As Regan (1984: 361–2) famously pointed out – in regard to
the position exemplified by Leopold, one which allows for
the sacrifice of individual interests in order to maintain the
value of the 'biotic community': 'It is difficult to see how
the notion of the rights of the individual could find a home
within a view that, emotive connotations to one side, might
be fairly dubbed "environmental fascism".' It is important
to recognize, in addition, that even the version of environmentalism that does not accept holistic value theory, but
merely recognises the value of ecosystems to individual
entities living within them, is problematic from an animal
rights/liberation perspective. This is because the sacrifice
of individual interests (including, presumably, those of
humans), is justified if the result is that the bulk of the
entities in any one ecosystem or species survives. In practice this has led, most notably, to support amongst ecocentrics for hunting, a practice which animal advocates regard
as morally unacceptable. Similarly, being a radical Green
does not necessitate being a vegetarian – and, indeed, meat
eating may be compulsory if it can be shown to be beneficial
to the overall well-being of the members of a species or an
ecosystem. Indeed, as Callicot (1995: 55) rightly points out:
'Meat eating may be more *ecologically* responsible than a
wholly vegetable diet' (although see below for his later conversion to vegetarianism).

The conflict between environmental holism and animal
protection individualism is played out most often in the
context of the debate about endangered species. If there is a
choice between saving a few members of an endangered
species or many more of a common species, an ecocentric
is likely to argue that ecological integrity demands the
former option (as indeed might an anthropocentric environmentalist concerned about the loss to humans of a particular
species). For an animal rights advocate, on the other hand,
the fact that some animals are members of an endangered
species is irrelevant, and the choice must be to save the
more populous group since by so doing more individual

rights are being protected. As Regan (1984: 359) points out: 'The rights view is a view about the moral rights of individuals. Species are not individuals, and the rights view does not recognise the moral rights of species to anything, including survival.' As a result, Regan continues, 'that an individual animal is among the last remaining members of a species confers no further right on that animal'. This is not to say that, for Regan, protecting endangered animals is unimportant, but it is important to appreciate the reason why it is important. Efforts to support endangered animals are important:

> not because these animals are few in number; primarily it supports them because they are equal in value to all who have inherent value, ourselves included, sharing with us the fundamental right to be treated with respect. (Regan, 1984: 360)

The failure of animal rights/liberation advocates to be prepared to sanction what environmentalists regard as ecologically necessary culling, then, has led the latter to criticize the former for being 'bunny-huggers', lacking in scientific rigour and too influenced by emotionalism. It would seem, then – to borrow from the title of Callicot's article (1995) – that the animal rights/liberation advocate faces two challengers – not only the traditional deniers of a higher moral status for animals (the 'ethical humanists') but also environmental ethicists – in a triangular controversy. Indeed, there is something in Callicot's claim (1995: 57–8) that animal rights/liberation advocates have more in common with the ethical humanists than the environmental ethicists, in the sense that both are 'firmly anchored to familiar paradigms', most notably an atomistic individualism which contrasts sharply with the 'holistic value theory' of at least some environmental ethicists.

The conflict between the holism of ecocentrism (and anthropocentric versions of environmentalism) and the individualism of animal rights/liberation/welfare, goes a long way towards explaining why the environmental and animal protection movements do not always see eye to eye, and why there is a limited crossover of membership. It is interesting to note, for instance, that they have very different origins. The environmental movement emerged to conserve the countryside as an amenity for humans to enjoy, and, later, the scientific importance of ecosystems. The animal protection movement, on the other hand, derives from the humane movements of the nineteenth century which tended, as we have seen in other chapters of this book, to be closely linked with other Victorian social reform movements concerned with such issues as slavery, child labour and women's emancipation, issues where the protection of the individual is the key motivation (Garner, 1993: chapter 2).

Conflict between the two movements has been endemic because of their differing traditions and values. Two examples will suffice here to illustrate this point. The first refers to the release of factory-farmed mink by animal liberation activists in Britain in 1998. Whilst this act was widely condemned by the conservation community because of its impact on the local ecosystem, animal liberationists were unrepentant because what concerned them was the liberation of exploited animals (*Daily Telegraph*, 10 August 1998). This also reflects the tendency amongst animal rights advocates to recommend a strategy of leaving nature to its own devices. As Regan (1984: 357) comments:

> Being neither the accountants nor managers of felicity in nature, wildlife managers should be principally concerned with *letting animals be*, keeping human predators out of their affairs, allowing these 'other nations' to carve out their own destiny.

The second example relates to an anecdote about the relationship between two of Britain's biggest, and best known, environmental and animal protection organisations, the Royal Society for the Protection of Birds (RSPB) and the Royal Society for the Prevention of Cruelty to Animals (RSPCA). In an interview with an RSPCA official (8 September 1994) I was told that the organization, ever conscious of its 'brand identity', was particularly annoyed that the RSPB was raising money for oil-stricken birds in the aftermath of a major spill. Not only was this a threat to the RSPCA's dominance in the animal welfare field (the public, apparently, regularly confuse the two organizations), but it was particularly galling in this case because of the way in which the two organizations were treating the affected birds, the RSPCA genuinely trying to clean the birds found whereas the RSPB, I was told – concerned more with species than individuals – were wringing their necks. One wonders what the public's reaction to this would have been.

Interestingly enough, in a similar vein, there are examples of conservation organization using the public's undoubted affinity with the protection of individual animals to fund a holistic policy. Perhaps the best example is the WWF's attempt to raise funds by persuading the public to 'adopt' wild animals from endangered species. To all intents and purposes, the public are given the impression that they are adopting individual animals, complete with names and regular progress reports. In reality, the funding is designed to protect the species, and little attention directed to individual animals which may or may not survive.

Finally, in this section, it should be noted that, as a consequence of the emphasis on the beauty and integrity of the natural world, there is a tendency in ecocentric thought to not only accept the moral acceptability of sacrificing individual wild animals, but also to have a contemptuous attitude towards domesticated animals, which are regarded as human artefacts having a negative impact on ecological diversity. The most extreme example of this is provided by Callicott (1995), in an article, originally published in 1980, described by one academic commentator as 'the single most influential paper written by an environmental ethicist on the subject of animal welfare' (Hargrove, 1992: xv–xvi) and by another as an essay which 'was remarkably influential within the environmental ethics community' (Jamieson, 1998: 44).

Callicot (1995: 50), following in the tradition of John Muir the nineteenth century American environmentalist who described sheep as 'hooved locusts', wrote that:

> Domestic animals are creations of man. They are living arte-facts, but artefacts nevertheless, and they constitute yet another mode of extension of the works of man into the ecosystem. From the perspective of the land ethic a herd of cattle, sheep, or pigs is as much or more a ruinous blight on the landscape as a fleet of four-wheel-drive off-road vehicles.

It is not the primary purpose of this chapter to critically examine the attitude towards domesticated animals of some ecocentric thinkers, rather than to explain how it departs from an animal protection ethic. Nevertheless, it is worth pointing out that Calicott's view (1995: 51) that it is 'literally meaningless' to 'liberate' domesticated animals because they do not have the behavioural repertoire to exist freely ('bred to docility, tractability, stupidity, and dependency' in Callicot's phrase) is to deny a great deal of evidence about their capabilities, a fact that Calicott recognizes in a later preface to his original essay (1995: 29–30).

A reconciliation?

From the above it ought to have become apparent that the exponents of environmental ethics – if we define its content in a narrow fashion – and animal rights/liberation hold significantly opposed views. Varner (1998: 98) goes as far as to say that 'most environmental philosophers believe that animal rights views are incompatible with sound environmental policy'. Not all ecocentrics, it should be said, promote the extreme holism of Leopold, celebrated most notably by Calicott, which denies the importance of individuals by attaching intrinsic value to collective entities such as ecosystems and species. One can agree here with Attfield's assertion (2003: 39) that 'no value-theory focusing entirely on the collective good rather than on that of individuals can even begin to be plausible'.

Nevertheless, as was pointed out earlier, even a more moderate environmentalism, fully cognisant of the value of individual animals, will usually regard sacrificing their interests as necessary to protect an ecosystem upon which individual animals depend. This, of course, is why environmentalists are more likely to recognize the value of hunting. There have been some attempts, however, to seek to reconcile ecocentrism with animal rights/liberation views. Indeed, even Callicot moderated his earlier position in an article originally published in 1988 (reprinted in Callicot, 1992) and in a preface to a reprint of his *Animal Liberation* piece (1995: 29–30), where he claims that animal rights/liberation views are closer to environmental ethics than he previously thought. Whilst these later works are shorn of much of the earlier rhetoric against the animal rights/

liberation position, however, it does not appear that much of substance has changed from his original critique.

Callicot does claim admittedly (1995: 30) that vegetarianism is now justified by the land ethic, but, as we shall see below, this is not based on animal rights/liberation grounds. Moreover, he is now prepared to admit that we do owe obligations to domesticated animals (1995: 29), and that we should treat them differently from wild animals on the grounds that they are members of a human/animal community 'and ought to enjoy ... all the rights and privileges, whatever they may turn out to be, attendant upon that membership' (1992: 257). What that means in practice, however, we are not really told. Furthermore, Callicot does not envisage any compromise with animal right/liberation advocates over the way in which wild animals are to be treated. Wild animals, he suggests (1992: 257), 'are members of the biotic community' and 'the structure of the biotic community is described by ecology', thereby, it seems, that the interests of individual wild animals can be sacrificed. It is clear that determining our moral obligations to animals, not by their characteristics but by the different functions they serve, is unacceptable to an animal rights/liberation advocate, and there would seem to be little evidence of convergence here.

A potentially more fertile ground for convergence is the implications of the recognition that extending moral considerability to non-sentient entities does not necessarily lead to an acceptance of what might be called biotic egalitarianism, whereby every part of nature is of equivalent value. As a result, preference can still be given to sentiency so that those with this characteristic have greater moral worth. As Fox (1984: 199) puts it: 'Cows do scream louder than carrots'. Attfield (2003: 44–6) develops such an hierarchical ethical system whereby humans, animals and living – but non-sentient – parts of nature all have moral standing but decreasing amounts of moral significance.

Insofar as ecologists do not reject totally the moral worth of sentiency, it is possible for animals to be given a privileged position within an ecocentric ethic. Not only might this avoid the sacrifice of animal interests in favour of those of non-sentient parts of nature, it also allows concern for the suffering of domesticated animals to emerge. As a reflection of this, it is usually the case that Green parties have animal welfare commitments far in advance of mainstream parties, particularly when they coincide with broader environmental objectives.

Despite the granting of a privileged position for sentient beings, however, an ethic – such as Attfield's – that awards moral standing to non-sentient entities within a hierarchical system of moral significance – is problematic, to say the least. Unanswered questions remain. In particular, it needs to be asked under what circumstances the interests of non-sentient entities would override those of sentient beings. If there are such circumstances, then what are they and what is left of the claim that sentient beings are privileged? Alternatively, if they never can override the interests of sentient beings then it seems meaningless to accord moral standing to non-sentient parts of nature in the first place, since their interests will only triumph when to do so coincides with the furtherance of those of sentient beings, or when the impact of so doing is neutral. This scenario appears to be little different to a sentient-centric ethic which accords extrinsic value to non-sentient entities only. It would appear, then, that for animal rights/liberation advocates, it is not good enough that sentiency is merely a sufficient condition for the possession of moral standing. It must be a necessary condition too, thereby ruling out the acceptability of an ecocentric or biocentric ethic.

There has also been some attempt to reconcile the holism of ecocentrism with the individualism of animal protection views. Most notably, Varner (1998) attempts to illustrate, mainly through the issue of hunting, that animal advocates can accept the deaths of some animals if by so doing other animals can prosper. Positions adopted by Regan and Singer, he suggests: 'in which pre-eminent value is ascribed to the lives of individual sentient creatures, can support hunting in every situation in which an environmentalist feels compelled to support it'. Varner's detailed argument is that the advocates of environmentalists and animal rights 'can agree on the moral necessity of therapeutic hunting of obligatory management species' (1998: 101). By therapeutic hunting, Varner means 'hunting motivated by and designed to secure the aggregate welfare of the target species, the integrity or health of its ecosystem, or both' (*ibid.*: 100). By obligatory management species, he means 'one that has a fairly regular tendency to overshoot the carrying capacity of its range', the paradigmatic case being the elephant (101).

Environmentalists, Varner continues, only need to support therapeutic hunting and can therefore oppose, as do animal rights advocates, hunting for sport. More contentiously, he also wants to suggest that animal rights advocates can also support therapeutic hunting. This, he believes, is possible if one strips away the sloganising and point-scoring and examine what animal advocate philosophers say in detail. He notes firstly (1998: 103–11) that Singer, as a utilitarian, can justify therapeutic hunting of obligatory management species on the grounds that it involves less pain than letting nature take its course. Varner recognizes that this assertion requires empirical confirmation, and it in part depends on the impracticality of using, as Singer suggests, non-lethal methods of population control.

I think it fair to conclude that utilitarianism may, or may not, permit hunting. This is nothing new in the sense that Singer has been regularly criticized by animal rights advocates, and particularly Regan, for not providing an ethic that will, in the vast majority of circumstances, prohibit morally meat eating and animal experimentation (Regan, 1984: chapter 6). But surely the rights theory itself cannot be used to justify hunting. Regan himself tackles this issue in *The Case for Animal Rights* (1984: 353–9). Here, the therapeutic case is rejected comprehensively. Regan questions whether the death endured by hunted animals is always preferable to death by starvation. But, in any case, he continues (356):

> No approach to wildlife can be morally acceptable if it assumes that policy decisions should be made on the basis of aggregating harms and benefits . . . Policies that lessen the total amount of harm at the cost of violating the rights of individuals . . . are wrong.

As a consequence:

> the goal of wildlife management should be to defend wild animals in the possession of their rights, providing them with the opportunity to live their own life, by their own lights, as best they can, spared that human predation that goes by the name of 'sport'. (357)

Varner for his part, despite recognizing Regan's opposition to hunting, is adamant that use of Regan's so-called 'miniride' principle could be employed to justify therapeutic hunting. According to Regan, when we have a choice between sacrificing the interests of the many who are innocent or the few who are innocent, the miniride principle compels us to choose the latter since this way more rights will be protected (Regan, 1984: 305–7). For Varner (1998: 113), the implications of this are clear. 'If it is true that fewer animals will die if therapeutic hunting is used to regulate a wildlife population than if natural attrition is allowed to take its course', he argues, 'then Regan's view implies that therapeutic hunting is not only permissible but a morally mandatory expression of respect for animals' rights.'

It is by no means clear that Varner has interpreted Regan's miniride principle correctly. Moreover, even if he has, a viable rights view is not, it seems to me, consistent with the sacrifice of animal interests involved in hunting, or in any other practice. On the first issue, there is a strong case for saying that the miniride principle does not apply to hunting because it is not a situation where a choice *has* to be made. Not acting, thereby leaving the animals alone – a decision which Regan urges us to take in the case of wild animals – is a neutral act. As Varner himself admits (1998: 114), 'while hunters would be responsible for the deaths of the animals they kill in a therapeutic hunt, no one would be responsible for deaths due to natural attrition'.

One way of showing how difficult it is to reconcile Varner's conclusions with a meaningful notion of rights is to substitute human for animals in the above arguments. Thus, would it be acceptable to cull innocent humans in a situation where overpopulation had become a problem threatening the well-being of others? Varner (1998: 115) argues it would not because 'it is possible for any normal adult human both to understand the gravity of the situation and to alter his or her behaviour accordingly'. But, the question remains, what if humans do not understand? Is culling permissible then? Varner's logic with regard to the treatment of animals in the hunting issue leads him to suggest that it is, and so he is forced to make the statement that: 'At some point ... some number of innocent human beings ought to be killed to prevent the foreseeable deaths of some larger number' (Varner, 1998: 115). Whatever one thinks of this statement, and it may or may not strike the reader as sensible, it surely cannot be made compatible with a rights view, if such a view is to make any sense at all.

An enlightened anthropocentrism

One final possible area of convergence between animal liberation/rights views and environmentalists in general is the possibility that the protection of human interests will, in many instances, necessitate pursuing policies which will coincide with the interests of animals *and* the environment. The philosophical and political difficulty of establishing this ecocentric ethic has led a number of Green political theorists to attempt to formulate an 'enlightened anthropocentrism' which, whilst recognizing the human-centred reality of the moral world, does claim to be consistent with a high degree of protection for nonhuman nature (J. Barry, 1999: chapters 2 and 3; Dobson, 2000; Hayward, 1995 and 1998; Norton, 1991; Vincent, 1995: 254–5). Such a case is based primarily on an empirical claim that the protection of the natural world, including animals, is in the interests of humans.

There is some evidence of a convergence between the human interests served by environmentalism and the protection of animals, and some instances where human interests in general are served by the protection of animals. In the latter case, for instance, the animal protection movement has made much of the claim that animal experimentation is invalid because it does not work, rather than because it is unethical (Garner, 1993: chapter 5). If evidence can be employed to show that using animals in the laboratory actually harms human interests – as is claimed with drugs, such as thalidomide, tested on animals but still causing detrimental effects when released on the market – then animal and human interests will coincide.

In the former case above, the environmental effects of factory farming is the best known example where a reform regarded as beneficial by anthropocentric environmentalism also has a positive animal welfare impact. The damage caused to the environment by factory farming is well-established (Mason and Singer, 1990: 72–127). More controversially, raising animals for meat under any system might be considered environmentally detrimental. Jamieson (1998: 46), commenting on the production and consumption of beef, sets out the full human costs. Not only is it a 'moral atrocity', he argues, but it also:

> causes health problems for consumers, reduces grain supplies for the poor, precipitates social divisions in developing countries, contributes to climate change, leads to the conversion of forests to pasture lands, is a causal factor in overgrazing, and is implicated in the destruction of native plants and animals.

As a result, Jamieson continues, 'if there is one issue on which animal liberationists should speak with a single voice it is on this issue'. This convergence of interests was recognised by Callicot (1995: 30) in his later, more conciliatory, phase. He had come to see that 'a vegetarian diet is indicated by the land ethic', since:

> Rainforests are felled to make pasture for cattle. Better for the environment if we ate forest fruits instead of beef. Livestock ruin watercourses and grasslands. And raising field crops for animal feed increases soil erosion and ground-water depletion.

Much the same critique of enlightened anthropocentrism in the broader environmental sphere (Garner, 2000) can be applied to its applicability to the protection of animal interests. In short, it is clearly inadequate from an animal liberation perspective. It can be readily agreed that, on occasions, the interests of humans and animals (and humans and nature more broadly) coincide. However, this relationship remains a contingent one, and there are many cases where protecting animals may serve no particular human interests or where, most significantly, there may be a conflict between upholding the interests of animals and those of humans. To give one pertinent example, environmentalists are very keen to ensure that chemicals are toxicity-tested extensively before they are permitted to be used. But of course this testing is undertaken largely on animals.

What makes the animal rights movement distinctive is that, like no anthropocentric cause, it requires the defence of nonhuman animal species, even when there is a human cost of so doing. This, of course, is precisely why an issue such as animal experimentation is politically contentious with exponents arguing that scientific procedures involving animals are vital for the advance of knowledge and advocates of animal rights denying the moral right of scientists to engage in it irrespective of the outcome. Only an ethic that postulates the intrinsic value of animals – divorced from the consequences to humans of protecting them – will therefore suffice if the radical aims of animal advocates are to be achieved, and this requirement is not acknowledged by an anthropocentric ethic, however enlightened it may be.

Far from offering us an appropriate ideological location for the protection of animal interests, this chapter has revealed that there are severe difficulties in the successful reconciliation of animal protection and environmentalism. This applies to both anthropocentric and ecocentric versions of environmentalism. Somewhat ironically, given the critique offered earlier in this book, we have found that the principles taken by animal rights/liberation advocates from liberal thought are very important defences against the holism and moral extensionism of ecocentric thought. Moreover, the protection afforded to animals within anthropocentric versions of environmentalism, while sometimes effective at a philosophical and strategic level, is ultimately unacceptably contingent upon a coincidence of interests which in many significant instances is not present.

Note

1 Some environmental philosophers want to limit the label 'environmental ethics' to apply only to positions which accord moral standing to the whole of the natural world, sentient and non-sentient (Thompson, 1990). I agree with Attfield (2003: 15–17) that such a definition, which would, of course, exclude animal rights/liberation views, is unduly restrictive.

7

Feminism and animals

'Should feminists be vegetarians?' asks Carol Adams (1993: 195), one of the foremost advocates of a feminist approach to animal ethics. More to the point, for the purposes of this book, should animal advocates be feminists? In other words, is feminism the most appropriate ideological location for the protection of animal interests? After documenting the very substantial role played by women in the animal protection movement, this chapter examines ecofeminism in general before evaluating the major arguments of those who seek to justify a feminist location for animal protection. It is suggested that the equating of female oppression with that of animals is unconvincing, and that feminists are, at the very least, premature in seeking to reject traditional rationalistic rights and utilitarian approaches in favour of an ethic of care.

The political sociology of women and animals protection

The theoretical attempt to link feminism with animal protection is accompanied by, and gets its main impetus from, the sociology of women's involvement in the animal protection movement. It is clear that women do play, and have historically played, an important role in the animal protection movement. Women's involvement, however, is more complex than this basic fact allows for.

From the nineteenth century women have been conspicuous in the animal protection movement. Many 'first-wave' feminists in Britain and the United States advocated vegetarianism and/or animal welfare reform. These included Mary Wollstonecraft, Harriet Beecher Stowe, Lydia Maria Child, Elizabeth Blackwell, Elizabeth Cady Stanton, Frances Willard, Caroline Earle White and Agnes Ryan (see Donovan, 1993: 188 n. 29 for details of their published work). Vegetarianism has historical links with feminism through the British suffrage movement, particularly its militant strand (Watkins, 1999: 11), and, for reasons that will be explored below, female participation was particularly prevalent in the anti-vivisection movement.

In the context of anti-vivisection, particular mention should be made of Frances Power Cobbe, who was co-founder, in 1875, of the Victoria Street Society for the Protection of Animals Liable to Vivisection, and later, in 1898, formed the British Union for the Abolition of Vivisection after disagreeing with the willingness of some members of the Victoria Street Society, which was renamed the National Antivivisection Society after the split, to compromize. Cobbe was an active feminist campaigning for female suffrage and was also concerned about the legal rights of women and the access of women to professions (Ferguson, 1998: 105–24). Also notable was the work of Anna Kingsford. One of the few women to qualify as a doctor in the late nineteenth century, she successfully completed her training (which included a thesis on the merits of vegetarianism) without witnessing vivisection, which she tirelessly campaigned against for the rest of her life (Elston, 1990: 276).

According to Elston (1990: 267), about 70 per cent of the Victoria Street Society's members between 1870 and 1900 were women, and they also constituted about 70 per cent of the RSPCA's membership in 1900. These figures do not necessarily paint an accurate figure since then, as now, many who generally support an organisation's objectives are reluctant, for a variety of reasons, to join. Inevitably, we are left reliant on impressionistic accounts. French (1975: 239–40) offers one when he writes that: 'if contemporary testimony is to be trusted, levels of female participation in the anti-vivisection movement would seem to have been among the very highest for movements without overtly feminist objectives'.

Evidence suggests that women predominate in the modern animal protection movement as much, if not more, than they do in the past. One American study conducted in the late 1980s, for instance, estimated that 70 per cent of the animal protection movement consisted of women (Rowan, 1989: 99–100). In Britain, similarly, one survey conducted at about the same time revealed that women are twice as likely to be vegetarians as men (Porritt and Winner, 1988: 197), and data provided by the International Fund for Animal Welfare a decade later revealed that no less than 72 per cent of its members are female (*Daily Telegraph*, 10 July 1997). My own research has also confirmed this female preponderance. In the early 1990s, women dominated the contact lists of some of the major British national organisations (containing volunteers acting for the organisation in local groups). No less than 62 of the 93 contacts of the National Antivivisection Society were women, and an even higher preponderance (68 out of 104 and 80 out of 103) occurred in Animal Aid and Compassion in World Farming respectively (Garner, 1993: 67).

Finally, it is also interesting to note that women's involvement with animal issues extends beyond the movement itself. For instance, primatology is the only area of science in which women outnumber men, constituting 62 per cent of members of the World Directory of Primatologists and running over 90 per cent of private sanctuaries (Jahme, 2000). Extremely well-known and well-regarded women in this area of study include Jane Goodall, who studies chimpanzees, and Dian Fossey, who devoted her life to gorillas.

The fact that there is a preponderance of women in the animal protection movement does not, by itself, indicate that gender plays a decisive role in this involvement. As will be shown below, some feminists deny the importance of the relationship between gender and animal protection. In the nineteenth century, to give one example, some prominent feminists – such as Elizabeth Garrett Anderson and Eleanor Sidgwick – were opposed to the campaign against vivisection (Elston, 1990: 263). A small-scale set of interviews with contemporary British female animal protection activists by Watkins (1999: 22, 31, 34) paints a mixed picture. One respondent argued strongly that gender was an important factor in her involvement, pointing out that: 'I can't understand why a feminist can't see the connection with the treatment of farm animals – cows having their calves taken away, pigs on rape racks, battery hens caged all their lives and used as egg producing machines.' Others, however, had less clear-cut views and none of those surveyed had heard of ecofeminism.

Another important point to make is that women in the past (Elston, 1990: 267–8) and contemporaneously are less prevalent in leadership positions than men within the animal protection movement. Gruen (1993: 81–2) notes, for instance, that at the March for Animals, the biggest demonstration of animal rights activists ever in the United States held in Washington DC in 1990, the vast majority of participants were women but very few of the platform speakers were women. As a counter to this, it should be pointed out that the animal protection movement has always contained some extremely able women in leadership positions, and, as for the public interest sector in general, as well as business, the under-representation of women in leadership positions in the animal protection movement may be being, to some degree, corrected. In the United States, for instance, a number of women have held high-profile positions within the animal protection movement, most notably Christine Stevens (the Animal Welfare Institute), Ingrid Newkirk (People for the Ethical Treatment of Animals), Holly Hazard (the Doris Day Animal League) and Adele Douglass (the American Humane Association). In Britain, similarly, leadership roles are held by Joyce D'Silva (Compassion in World Farming), Jackie Ballard (the first women to hold the position of Director General of the RSPCA) and Jan Creamer (National Antivivisection Society).

In addition, whilst it is broadly true that women do predominate in the animal protection movement, the vast majority of women are not animal advocates, and are not even vegetarians. As Donovan (1993: 168) confirms:

> while women have undoubtedly been less guilty of active abuse and destruction of animals than men . . . they nevertheless have been complicit in that abuse, largely in their use of luxury items that entail animal pain and destruction (such as furs) and in their consumption of meat.

Of course, this does not show in itself that feminism, as an ideology, is an inappropriate location for animal protection,

only that some individual women do not support the objectives of animal protectionists.

Finally in this section, it should be noted that women's
involvement in the animal protection movement has not
precluded it from accusations of sexism. Francione (1996:
74) has claimed that 'in recent years, the promotion of
animal causes has increasingly relied on sexist and racist
imagery'. Whilst this is probably an exaggeration, the use
of sexist images, particularly in the anti-fur campaign, has
been noticeable. David Bailey's adverts for the British anti-
fur group Lynx often criticised the women who wear fur
with derogatory language as in the 'Poor bitch. Rich bitch'
example. In the United States, there have been more extreme examples. Adams (1994: 134), for instance includes a
photograph of the anti-fur advert which read 'it takes up to
40 dumb animals to make a fur coat; but only one to wear
it', defaced by feminists who wrote on it 'Men kill animals
... Men make the profits ... and Men make sexist ads'.
People for the Ethical Treatment of Animals, in particular,
have not been slow in utilizing female glamour to 'sell'
animal protection messages. In the 1990s, for instance, it
used supermodels to promote its 'I'd rather go naked than
wear fur' campaign, as well as joining forces with *Playboy*
magazine in a campaign to increase organ donation thereby
reducing the reliance on animals (Francione, 1996: 74–6).

Ecofeminism

As was intimated earlier, the fact that a large proportion of
women eat animals and support animal experimentation
does not condemn feminism from an animal protection
perspective. Equally, however, the fact that women are so-
ciologically important to the animal protection movement
does not mean, of course, that feminism is theoretically
useful to the protection of animals. The rest of this chapter
will be an attempt to evaluate the claim that feminism is
ideologically important for the protection of animal interests. There is now a fairly extensive feminist literature on
animal rights, which is a sub-sector of similar arguments
employed in the more general eco-feminist field. From this

perspective, 'Androcentrism, not anthropocentrism, is the chief enemy of women and nature' (Tong, 1998: 251). Although, as we saw, concern for animals in feminist thought has a long history, animal protection is far from being universally acknowledged as a feminist issue (Gruen, 1993: 75–7). Somewhat ironically, given the problems for animal protection of the tendency of liberals to adopt moral pluralism detailed earlier in this book, many feminists have argued against imposing restraints on our treatment of animals (such as making vegetarianism morally compulsory for feminists) on the grounds of a commitment to pluralism. As Adams (1993: 195), who has long sought to make meetings of women's organizations vegetarian affairs, explains, many feminists have sought to deny this by defending 'personal choice as an arbiter of ethical decisions and limits pluralistic concerns to those of oppressed human beings'.

Theoretical attempts to incorporate animal protection as a feminist issue are part of a broader eco-feminist strand. Although even some eco-feminists marginalize or reject a concern for individual animals, those who seek to promote a feminist concern for animals would regard themselves as eco-feminists. It was extremely likely, if not inevitable, that the link between women and animals was made. This is not just because women tend to predominate in the animal protection movement, but is primarily because, as Adams and Donovan (1995: 1) point out: 'the ideological justification for women's alleged inferiority has been made by appropriating them to animals; from Aristotle on, women's bodies have been seen to intrude upon their rationality', thereby preventing full membership of the moral community. Instead, historically in western culture women have been regarded as in between men and beasts, or, as in the title of the book by Adams (1994), neither man nor beast.

Feminists have tended to respond in one of two main ways to the common link drawn between women and nonhuman nature. Some feminists reject the attempt to ally women with nature, on the grounds that to emphasize women's biological closeness to nature is to reinforce claims that women are unequal to men who are associated with reason and culture (see Plumwood, 1993). Emphasizing the distinct humaneness of women is the consequence of this response. Thus, it is ironic that Mary Wollstonecraft, the author, in 1792, of the famous feminist tract *Vindication of the Rights of Women*, was ridiculed by the Cambridge philosopher Charles Taylor, who responded with his *Vindication of the Rights of Brutes*. For Taylor, giving rights to women, identified closely with nature, on the grounds that they possessed reason, was as preposterous as giving rights to nonhuman animals. Little wonder, then, that Wollstonecraft, as some modern feminists do, sought to deny that women, in Elston's words (1990: 260–1):

> were more governed by their passions than men, and, therefore closer to nature ... If reason was what distinguished man ... from brutes, women had it no less than men. Women, therefore, were distinct from 'brutes', they had moral autonomy and moral rights.

The second, classically ecofeminist, response is to embrace the women/nature connection in order to see the true source of women's oppression, and therefore their liberation (see Griffin, 1978). Those ecofeminists who emphasize the shared oppression of women and animals in particular argue, as Adams and Donovan (1995: 5) explain, that: 'Just as the imputed animality of women precluded our inclusion in the political community, so a great deal of exploitation and abuse of animals is legitimized by feminizing them.' To liberate animals, therefore, is to liberate women and *vice versa*.

Ecofeminists tend to see the oppression of animals as one of many interlinked forms of oppression. The following passage from Gaard (1993a: 5) is a particularly extreme example. 'By documenting the poor quality of life for women, children, people in the Third World, animals and the environment', she writes:

> ecofeminists are able to demonstrate that sexism, racism, classism, speciesism, and naturism (the oppression of nature) are mutually reinforcing systems of oppression. Instead of being a 'single-issue' movement, ecofeminism rests on the notion that the liberation of all oppressed groups must be addressed simultaneously.

Ecofeminists, therefore, seek to remove what they perceive to be the 'category of "otherness"' (Gruen, 1993: 80) found in other theories, including liberal and radical versions of feminism, in favour of inclusivity and the ending of all oppression.

Such an approach, strongly reminiscent of the grand narratives that some feminists would condemn as masculine, is surely overly simplistic. For one thing, it denies the reality that individuals, often coalescing into groups, have competing interests that the state has to seek to reconcile. These conflicts may be based on gender but, equally as likely, they will be based on class, nation, or race. Moreover, the suggestion that many forms of oppression can be solved simultaneously by the promotion of ecocentric ethics exaggerates the degree to which the interests of different oppressed groups are compatible. In the case of the passage from Gaard, for instance, it is by no means clear that protecting the interests of animals is necessarily compatible with the interests of people in the developing world, or for that matter with the environment. As we saw in the previous chapter, to give one example, protecting individual elephants or rhinos is not seen by some as the best way of preserving the species as a whole. Likewise, allowing animal populations to grow uncontrolled is not in the interests of those humans seeking to make a living from the land.

Feminism and the protection of animals

Although the arguments, as befits an ideology which prides itself on its diversity, have been varied, there tend to be two main themes in the discourse seeking to demonstrate that feminism and animal protection are inextricably linked. The first might be described as the 'oppression' argument in the sense that it seeks to show that 'sexism and speciesism are interconnected, mutually reinforcing systems of oppression and ways of organizing the world'. The second theme is an attempt to employ an 'ethic of care' as an alternative to rights-based theories of justice (Adams, 1996: 174).

The first, oppression, theme suggests that women are and have been victims of patriarchy in the same ways that animals have. Adams and Donovan (1995: 7) again articulate this view well when they write that:

Women must not deny their historical linkage with animals but rather remain faithful to them, bonded as we are not just by centuries of similar abuse but also by the knowledge that they – like us, often objectified as Other – are subjects worthy of the care, the respect, even the reverence, that the sacredness of consciousness deserves.

What does this 'similar abuse' amount to? In the first place, Adams (1990), the most prolific exponent of an animal protection strand of feminism, has written extensively about the relationship between the meat industry and patriarchy. The fact that derogatory terms applied to women – 'slabs of meat', 'bitch', 'cow', 'sow' – have animal origins, indicates the shared low esteem both have in a male-dominated culture (Dunayer, 1995). A shared sense of oppression is also provided by the fact that female animals tend to suffer more in intensive agriculture than male ones. Some of the worst examples of 'factory' farming – the battery cage, sow tethers and stalls, the intensive use of cows – involve female animals, and the production and consumption of 'feminised protein' (Adams, 1993: 197) provides perhaps the most prominent example of gender affinity between women and animals. Moreover, meat eating itself is perceived to be a masculine pursuit, linked as it is – inaccurately of course – with providing the strength that men need to do demanding manual work. It is suggested that whenever there is a shortage of meat in a patriarchal culture, it is women who go without (Gruen, 1993: 74).

The link between violence to women and violence to animals is another shared source of oppression. Not only are violent men likely to be violent to other humans and animals, but there is also evidence that men often use violence to the companion animals of their partners as a form of women-battering. As Adams (1995: 78) points out, 'harm to animals is a strategic expression of masculine power and can be found throughout male controls over women'.

From the nineteenth century, vivisection, at least in the eyes of many feminists, became inextricably linked with various indignities imposed upon women. It was connected, for instance, with the treatment meted out to militant suffragists so that, in Lansbury's words (1985: 24), 'the image of the vivisected dog blurred and became one with the militant suffragette being force fed in Brixton prison'. A more

long-standing source of common oppression is the treatment meted out to women and animals by the medical profession. This was particularly prevalent in the late nineteenth
century, although there are still echoes today, particularly
in the way that women's reproductive systems have been
subject to experiment in the developing world where, for
instance, hormonal contraceptives have been unethically
tested (Foster, 1995; Gruen, 1993: 66–9).

Doctors in general were criticised by the nineteenth
century anti-vivisection movement, particularly for their
treatment of poor women. Gynaecology was a new and
undeveloped discipline. Death rates from ovariotomies were
high, and portrayed by the anti-vivisection movement as a
symbol of the medical profession's disregard for women
and femininity itself (Elston, 1990: 278–9). In addition, the
anti-vivisection movement particularly allied itself against
the Contagious Diseases Acts which established state regulation of prostitution in garrison towns. Enforced medical
inspections were carried out on women suspected of prostitution, and those found to have sexually-transmitted diseases
had their liberty removed (Elston, 1990: 274).

The second, ethic of care, theme suggests that liberal accounts of animal rights or animal liberation are flawed because
they rely on arguments based upon rationality, logical consistency, universality, fairness and competitive adversarial
relationships. Although not accepted universally by feminists,
the caring ethic 'has been widely discussed and adopted within
feminist literature as a moral voice distinctive to women'
(Squires, 1999: 144). A critique of the traditional animal
rights/liberation approaches exemplified by Singer and Regan
would, from the care perspective, suggest that their:

> theoretical similarities are as significant as their differences. In
> particular, both . . . (of their approaches) are developed within a
> framework of patriarchal norms, which includes the subordina-
> tion of emotion to reason, the privileging of abstract principles
> of conduct, (and) the perception of ethical discussion as a battle
> between adversaries. (Luke, 1995: 291–2)

Luke's final point here is particularly important. Eco-
feminists condemn rights-based ethics above all because of
its assumption of competition and separateness. As Gaard,
1993a: 2), points out, rights-based ethics 'evolve from a sense
of self as separate, existing within a society of individuals

who must be protected from each other in competing for scarce resources'.

Feminists point to the rationalistic language of Singer and Regan, and their apparent eschewing of emotion. In the preface to *Animal Liberation* (1990: iii), for instance, Singer states that his book 'makes no sentimental appeals for sympathy toward "cute" animals' but rather is 'an attempt to think through, carefully and consistently, the question of how we ought to treat nonhuman animals ... Nowhere in this book ... do I appeal to the reader's emotions where they cannot be supported by reason', and the application of moral principles to the treatment of animals is 'demanded by reason, not emotion'. Regan, similarly, points out (1984: xii) that:

> Since all who work on behalf of the interests of animals are more than a little familiar with the tired charges of being 'irrational', 'sentimental', 'emotional' or worse, we can give the lie to these accusations only by making a concerted effort not to indulge our emotions or parade our sentiments. And that requires making a sustained commitment to rational inquiry.

Such language – perceived as essentially male – is problematic for feminist animal protectionists because it replicates those human characteristics that are used to justify moral superiority over animals. Instead, this discourse should be replaced, it is argued, by a 'care ethic', associated in particular with the work of Gilligan (1982), which privileges what are perceived to be essentially female values such as compassion, empathy sympathy, and context. This, it is argued, constitutes a much more appropriate language for animal advocates than rationality and justice. As Donovan (1993: 185) eloquently states:

> Out of a woman's relational culture of caring and attentive love ... emerges the basis for a feminist ethic for the treatment of animals. We should not kill, eat, torture, and exploit animals because they do not want to be so treated, and we know that. If we listen, we can hear them.

An evaluation

Should animal advocates be feminists? At the very least, this section will argue, we should exercise caution here. In the first place, the oppression argument, which sees parallels in the oppression of women and animals, only takes us so far. It is, of course, true that women are the victims of a shocking amount of male-induced violence, not least in the sado-masochism prevalent in the pornography industry, as well as the domestic environment where women are too often victims of abuse. It is true too that the patriarchal language sometimes used to describe women – as 'meat', 'cows', 'bitches' and so on – is animalistic and exploitative.

However, despite the undoubted violence exercized towards women by men, to equate it with the exploitation of animals is, at the very least, problematic. In the first place, exploiting animals is by no means a male preserve. It is true that a significant proportion of vegetarians and animal rights activists are women but, as we have seen, some are men and the vast majority of women are neither. Secondly, animals are, in every society in the world to varying degrees, exploited on a scale that has no parallels in the treatment of women. Moreover, the law in most societies prohibits violence to women whereas the law specifically allows violence to be visited on animals. Equating vivisection with women's experience of the medical profession, as many feminists have sought to do, is surely not a satisfactory comparison. Animals are routinely exploited in the laboratory for the benefit of men (and women). The animals used in this way do not benefit at all from what is done to them, and indeed usually pay with their lives, after suffering varying degrees of pain and distress.

Applying the feminist care ethic to animals is also problematic. In the first place, the critique of the rationalistic animal rights/liberation approaches is misplaced on a number of levels. Firstly, the emphasis placed by Singer and Regan on reason over emotion is a political strategy as much as it is an intellectual conviction. Here, they are right to suggest that, whatever the inherent merits of the case, arguments based on reason, logical consistency, rationality and so forth are more likely to curry favour with the public (in this particular issue area at least) than those based on care and compassion. Singer (1990: iii) recognises this, stating that: 'The portrayal of those who protest against cruelty to animals as sentimental, emotional "animal lovers" has had the effect of excluding the entire issue of our treatment of nonhumans from serious political and moral discussion.'

The feminist care ethic, of course, should not be seen as being based on emotion and sentiment, or certainly not exclusively so. Politically, however, the distinction between an ethic of care and arguments focusing on emotion and sentiment is much more difficult to sustain. Whatever the intellectual merits of the feminist account of animal ethics, then, it would be politically problematic for the animal protection movement to be associated with values such as emotion and sentiment. One has to recognize here what the animal protection movement is up against. Spinoza's comment (quoted in Midgley, 1983: 10) that 'it is plain that the law against the slaughtering of animals is founded rather on vain superstition and womanish pity than on sound reason' is but an exaggerated version of the taunt often faced by animal advocates, and against which the rationality of much animal ethics has been an effective counter.

Secondly, it is a mistake to suggest that rights/liberation approaches are entirely devoid of feelings of care, sympathy and compassion. Surely, this dichotomy is too stark. One cannot read Singer's *Animal Liberation*, for instance, without being moved by the animal suffering depicted in words and pictures which Singer himself hopes (1990: iii) will produce 'emotions of anger and outrage, coupled with a determination to do something about the practices described'. Donovan (1996: 38), it should be said, admits that Singer's utilitarianism is preferable to a rights-based approach anyway because it privileges sentiency over rationality, although she still remains opposed to its reliance on a rationalistic form of measurement.

In addition, despite the element of truth in Luke's assertion (1995: 193) that Regan's *Case for Animal Rights* 'is totally devoid of concrete references to feelings or experience', his other work does reveal that his ultimate motive for promoting the rights of animals is based around strongly held values of care and compassion. Regan's description of his conversion to animal rights, described in an autobiographical essay, is instructive here (1987: 27–8). Here, Regan described how the death of a much-loved companion animal contributed to his transformation into an advocate for animal rights. This, as he points out, was 'an affair of the heart, not the head'. Following the dog's death, Regan and Nancy, his partner, 'lapsed into a period of intense, shared grief' and it became apparent to him that his 'powerful feelings for this particular dog ... had to reach out to include other dogs' and, indeed, every other animal. 'From this point forward', he continues:

> my heart and head were one ... Philosophical argument can take the heart to the river, but perhaps it is only experience that can make it drink. The intellectual challenge before me was to try to make this sense of the world less vague and the grounds for accepting it rationally more compelling.

One can agree with Francione (1995a: 151–2) then that there is nothing inherently patriarchal about the concept of rights. Moreover, rights theory itself is not as cold and impersonal as some feminists claim, since it is built on respecting individuals, recognizing the harm that can befall them, and seeking to alleviate it. Insofar as rights theory 'presumes a society of equal autonomous agents, who require little support from others, who need only that their space be protected from other's intrusions' (Donovan and Adams, 1996: 15), it may be problematic from an animal protection perspective. This is particularly the case with domesticated animals that often need human intervention to improve their well-being. A negative version of rights, however, is not the only kind that can be adopted. Just as social and economic rights can be applied to humans, rights requiring human intervention to improve the welfare of animals are equally permissible.

The ethic of care approach is not an approach universally accepted by feminists, and may not be a moral position exclusively, or even predominantly, upheld by women. Indeed, as Squires (1999: 148) points out: 'There have been many empirical studies that question the simplicity of the equation of justice and care with men and women. Some have revealed class and race to be equally, if not more, significant variables.' It may be then that an ethic of care tends to be a factor in the culture of all marginalized groups rather than being gender specific (Squires, 1999: 145–6). If this is correct, we would be forced to limit the focus on feminism as the appropriate ideological location for animal protection, and look more widely at these other groups.

Despite this, contextualising animal suffering in particular circumstances is undoubtedly enriching and there is much value in Kheel's assertion (1996: 27) that 'If we *think*, for example, that there is nothing morally wrong with eating meat, we ought perhaps to visit a factory farm or slaughterhouse to see if we still *feel* the same way.' Gruen (1993: 79) makes essentially the same point, arguing that on strategic grounds it is important that the, often grim, reality of animal exploitation is directly experienced by more people. As she writes: 'As long as the theories that advocate the liberation of animals rely on abstraction, the full force of these consequences will remain too far removed to motivate a change in attitude.'

Only the hardest amongst us cannot fail to be moved by descriptions of what happens to animals is such places. Scully (2002: 128), the American conservative writer, passionately asks us to imagine:

> the bright, sensitive pig dangling by a rear hoof as he or she is processed along, squealing in horror; the veal calf taken from his mother, tethered and locked away in a tiny dark stall for all of his brief, wretched existence. If you could walk all of humanity through one of these places, 90 percent would never touch meat again. We would leave the place retching and gasping for air.

And again, quoting an interview with an abattoir worker in Washington state whose job is to cut off the hooves of strung-up cattle passing by at 309 an hour (*ibid.*: 284):

> When they reach him, they are supposed to be stunned and killed already, but often they're not, as Mr Moreno tells it. 'They blink. They make noises. The head moves, the eyes are open and still looking around. They die piece by piece'.

Against this emphasis on context rather than abstraction, however, there is the point that an ethic of care, unlike a theory of justice based on rights, provides little guide as to how we would universalize an individual experience to appeal to those who have not had that particular experience. As Regan (1991: 95–6) remarks:

> What are the resources within the ethic of care that can move people to consider the ethics of their dealings with individuals who *stand outside* the existing circle of their valued interpersonal relationships? . . . Unless we supplement the ethic of care with some other motivating force – some other grounding of our moral judgment – we run the grave risk that our ethic will be excessively conservative and will blind us to those obligations we have to people for whom we are indifferent.

Luke (1996: 86) rightly suggests that Regan's arguments here are predicated on a pessimistic assessment of people's willingness to care for animals and desire to protect them. This, of course, is an empirical question, and, given the abuse suffered by animals, it is difficult to challenge, other than anecdotally as Luke does, Regan's pessimism.

In general terms too, it is not clear how a society based on an ethic of care would manage disputes. As Francione (1995a: 151) remarks, in a passage reminiscent of a critique of Marx's apparent optimism about a benign human nature in a communist society:

> In a diverse and highly populous political system, there must be some mechanism that can be used to resolve the inevitable conflicts that will arise among individuals, irrespective of whether the society in question is matriarchal or patriarchal.

A related criticism is that an ethic of care does not provide us with much of a guide to action in general. For example, an animal rights perspective rules out meat eating as morally wrong, or does so if, like Regan, we apply a right to life to animals. It is not clear, by contrast, whether or not an ethic of care brings us to the same conclusion. As Manning (1996: 119) admits, it could be consistent with vegetarianism but on the other hand 'it is possible to give an animal care that is sensitive to its interests up to the moment of slaughter'. The vagueness of an ethic of care is particularly problematic when it is recognized that care works both ways in the animals debate. For instance, as defenders of animal experimentation have been increasingly vocally pointing out, the *care* of humans – men and women, adults and children – is dependent on animal research. In such a conflict of caring whose interests should we choose to uphold? Whilst an animal rights position has a clear answer to this question – that there may be gains from animal research but these gains are illegitimate because ill-gotten – an ethic of care has no such guiding principle.

The problem of ethical guidance is one reason for seeking to unite the care ethic with the rights/liberation positions. Indeed, as Squires (1999: 149) correctly observes, 'the overwhelming majority of feminist theorists have actually been keen to reconcile the two ethics in some way'. This involves a recognition that traditional notions of justice can form part of a caring ethic. By so doing, we are left with a much diluted feminist impact on animal protection, whereby traditional liberal-based notions of rights and utility are embellished, rather than replaced, by feminist insights into care and shared oppression. With this thought in mind, coupled with the arguments presented in the preceding chapters, maybe we are now in a position to conclude on the most appropriate ideological location for those who seek to protect the interests of animals.

Conclusion

This book began life as a critique of the liberal approach to animal protection, as well as an attempt to provide a general account of the impact on political theory of the incorporation of animal interests. In answer to the second of these tasks it is concluded that the incorporation of animal interests into political thinking does not challenge the conceptual morphology or structure of political theory in the sense that, if a higher moral status for animals is accepted, a new political language will have to be adopted or new, or previously marginalized, concepts emphasized. However, the incorporation of animal interests as more or less equivalent to those of humans does have a profound impact on the distribution of benefits deriving from otherwise unchanged political concepts. It is in this latter sense that animal liberation has far-reaching implications for the future of humans, as well as animals.

The implication of criticizing liberalism is that we should look elsewhere to find an appropriate ideological home for the protection of animal interests. Elements of other political traditions – the conservative notions of responsibility and paternalism, the communitarian perfectionist emphasis on a goal-based state with a shared moral code, the socialist goal of protecting the weak, a feminist care ethic, or the non-anthropocentric starting point of ecologism – would all potentially seem to offer us an alternative, and maybe stronger, basis for protecting animals. Somewhat surprisingly, though, a detailed consideration of these possible alternatives has revealed significant doubts about their ability to incorporate animal protection effectively. The main conclusion then is that, whilst the utilization of liberalism as an ally of animals does raise a number of serious problems, not least relating to the question of agency, it still remains preferable – embellished, perhaps, with elements from other ideological traditions – to the alternatives. A detailed exploration of what this embellished liberal theory of animal protection would look like will have to wait for a future occasion, but a number of suggested avenues of inquiry are indicated below.

The impact of animal rights on political theory

The emergence of a greater concern to protect the interests of animals has had an impact on the nature of political ideologies and political thinking in general. As we have seen, however, it has not so much impacted on the conceptual structure of ideologies as on their coverage. That is to say exponents of competing ideologies have sought to incorporate animal interests by extending the use of conceptual arrangements common to the ideology in question.

Liberals seek to extend the notions of rights, liberty and the social contract; an animal advocate seeking to utilize communitarianism would invoke shared moral values; Marxists seek to show how the limitations of rights discourse impacts upon vulnerable animals as much as it does upon vulnerable humans; conservatives seek to protect animals against the ravages of rationalistic science and technology; and feminists focus on showing how an ethic of care is a preferable vehicle for animal protection than a rationalistic rights or utilitarian account. Ecology is the only ideology that has at its core a non-anthropocentric ethic, and has not, as a result, had to extend its coverage. The incorporation of a concern for animal interests at the individual level has not been without its problems, however, and some thinkers deny its compatibility with a genuine environmental ethic.

Despite ideological morphology remaining virtually untouched by the challenge of nonhuman interests, their incorporation into ideologies still has a profound impact and, if accepted, requires a significant reconfiguration of conceptual analysis. Those who seek to promote the interests of animals and nature have challenged the presumption that political theory is about the 'human question'. In this sense, by extending enlightenment principles of justice, freedom, equality and rights across the species barrier, animal rights or liberation is the culmination of the modernist project. Previously, modernism has been essentially anthropocentric, designed to promote and secure human dominion over nature. This humanism has applied to 'all major western faiths and ideologies ... Christianity, Marxism, the manifold kinds of liberalism, the positivist faith of scientific fundamentalists' who all 'think of humans as being ... the currently dominant animal species ... (and) all think of the earth as a resource in the service of the human enterprise' (Gray, 1997: 159).

As a result of extending political concepts to include animals, modernism is fundamentally transformed since it inevitable results in human privileges being reduced. As Gray (1997: 173) accurately comments, 'A commitment to the earth entails a large deflation of human hopes.' Thus, 'expanding the circle' as Singer (1983) puts it will require political theorists to consider what it means to say that animals have rights against humans, freedoms from humans and equality with humans. Likewise, the recognition that animals have important interests raises questions about how, and by whom, those interests are to be represented.

Accepting the legitimacy of incorporating animal interests into the centre of ideological discourse also alters permanently the way in which ideologies are characterized. As Hamilton (1987: 18–38) points out, the definitional criteria of an ideology includes an association with *either* a particular group, class or collectivity within the wider society *or* with the whole society or community. This community, if we accept a theory of global social justice, might not be the nation state (Brown, 1998). If we accept that animals should be beneficiaries of political ideologies, however, then any ideology not including them ceases to have any claim to be a collective and universal ideology and instead becomes a sectional one designed to promote the interests of humans. Significantly, this also applies to theories of global social justice which, from an anthropocentric perspective, offer a Hegelian vision of a universal world community, but become equally partial if a case is made for the inclusion of animal interests.

Liberalism, property and moral pluralism

The first part of this book sought to examine liberalism's claims to be the most appropriate ideological location for the protection of animal interests, a not surprising place to start given, as we saw in chapter 1, the predominance of justifications for animal moral considerability from within the liberal tradition. In chapter 2, the property status of animals within liberal thought was considered as a possible obstacle to the achievement of a significant protection of animal interests. It was suggested that the negative impact on animals of their property status can, contrary to the opinion of a number of animal law scholars, be exaggerated, as can the benefits of changing the legal status of animals.

Two main dimensions to this contention were suggested. The first is the argument that abolishing the property status of animals is not a sufficient guarantee that they will cease to be exploited. The second is that, whilst the abolition of animals' property status is a necessary step towards the fulfilment of an animal rights agenda, it is incorrect to suggest that significant improvements to their well being cannot be achieved from within the existing property paradigm. This error is, partly at least, a product of a failure to recognize that the degree to which the welfare of animals can be sustained and improved is not a determinant of their legal status but is a product of first order political factors, and not least the prevailing ideological climate. Where the ideological climate is dominated by classical liberalism, as tends to occur in the United States rather more than in Britain, there is a greater reluctance to intervene in property rights. In so far as this analysis is correct, the target of those animal law scholars who comment on the negative implications of the property status of animals should be redirected to the real cause of the problem, that is the dominance of classical liberalism.

It was also noted in chapter 2 that achieving a widespread acceptance of a higher moral status for animals is, for a variety of reasons, unlikely to happen at the present time. The problem with this, as discussed in chapter 3, is that deprived of inclusion within a liberal system of rights or a non-speciesist utilitarian calculation, animals can find themselves, in both theory and practice, excluded from a liberal theory of justice and, consequently, victims of a moral pluralism central to liberal political thought.

It was also suggested in chapter 3 that Rawls' particular brand of liberal contractarian political theory is, illegitimately, inimical to the protection of animal interests. Rawls excludes animals as beneficiaries of his theory of distributive justice, not because this is the objective outcome of the deliberations in the original position, but because he brings to the debate challengeable assumptions about the determination of moral agency. As a result, while it can be shown, primarily through the argument from marginal cases, that attempts have been made to incorporate animals into his contractarian theory, this can only be done by bringing to the debate alternative assumptions about the determination of moral status. This nullifies the claim that a contractarian route to a high moral status for animals is preferable to the more traditional rights and utilitarian approaches.

Given these perceived weaknesses of liberal thought, from the perspective of animal protection, advocates for a higher moral status for animals would seem to be left with two options; either to continue aligning themselves with a liberal democratic political and theoretical framework, persisting with the claim that a higher moral status can and should be accorded to animals from within this tradition, or to dispense with the liberal tradition and a search for a more effective ideological fit begun. This latter option was pursued in chapters 4–7.

Liberalism embellished

A review of the compatibility with animal protection of various alternatives to liberalism reveals that none of them are entirely satisfactory. Significantly, too, by identifying the weaknesses of competing ideologies, liberalism's claim to be the most appropriate ideological location for animal protection looks stronger. A number of features of liberalism add to this strength. Firstly, the fact that liberalism has a central place within Western societies puts it at a distinct advantage over ideologies such as socialism, feminism and ecology, all of which tend to be oppositional rather than mainstream in the developed world.

Secondly, liberalism's universalism is more appropriate than the particularism of communitarianism and some feminisms which would seem to justify the present scenario where the treatment of animals varies enormously from country to country. Furthermore, the liberal focus on individualism is more consistent with the protection of individual animals than is the holism of ecology and the emphasis placed upon the well-being of collectivities such as species or ecosystems. Finally, the negative implications for animals of moral pluralism can be countered by incorporating them in a theory of justice so that, adapting Mill's harm principle, causing unnecessary harm to animals becomes morally illegitimate.

So, it appears, the wheel has turned full circle. For, against the particularity of communitarianism, the anthropocentrism of socialism, the holism of environmentalism and the vagueness of feminism, the universalism, individualism and precision of liberalism does not look at all bad. However, despite the weaknesses, from an animal protection perspective, of the ideological alternatives to liberalism, they do offer potentially important embellishments that might improve the ability of liberalism to defend the interests of animals. A detailed account of such a reformulated, animal friendly, liberalism requires further research and, perhaps, another book-length study. For now, what would seem to be the most important issues can be sketched.

The first issue to raise is a question mark against the ability of unfettered, free-market, liberalism to protect animal interests (and indeed human interests too). Institutionalized animal exploitation – in contract laboratories and factory farms – is not inherently capitalist in orientation. In liberal democratic societies, however, the bulk of animal exploitation does take place in the private sector, involving a considerable amount of capital investment and the generation of substantial profits. Coupled with this is the sanctity, within free market societies, of private property, which makes state intervention to regulate what is done to animals, regarded as property, difficult.

A related issue is that it is extremely difficult to justify greater equality between humans and animals if there is considerable inequality between humans, whether on the basis of class or gender. A liberalism which is intent upon protecting the interests of animals (and, some would suggest, many humans too) must, therefore, seek to reduce exploitation and increase equality. The best means of justifying this goal from a liberal perspective is on the grounds that it increases the liberty of both humans and animals. Here, too, values such as compassion, caring and cooperation, which socialists and many feminists share, would seem to be particularly relevant as a justification for reducing inequality and exploitation. Whether such values can be incorporated into a liberal theory of animal protection is, and must remain for now, an open question.

Another theme relates to the anthropocentric nature of liberalism. We have seen that liberalism can be rescued from the charge that it is an inappropriate ideological position for those who want to protect the interests of animals only if they can be incorporated within a liberal theory of justice. Equality between the species within such a theory of justice, demanded by animal rights and liberation advocates, can only be achieved, however, by a paradigm shift in liberal political and moral thought. What is required is an acceptance of the radical view, exemplified by dark green ecological thinking, that humans should not be regarded as the centre of the moral universe. Even if it is accepted that animals are inferior morally to humans, it is still necessary, if a viable form of animal welfarism is to emerge, to challenge the kind of hard-nosed anthropocentrism that trivialises and minimises the interests of animals. It might be the case that a more enlightened anthropocentrism can only come about if the rationalistic edges of liberalism are rounded. Here again, the eco-feminist insight that a viable theory of justice must have at its core notions of care and compassion might just do the trick here.

There is much work to be done, then, if liberalism is to be transformed into an ideology that can be accepted by those who want the interests of animals to be protected. The political economy of liberalism will have to be tempered by principles of state intervention and greater equality. These principles are not alien to liberalism, since they were part of a 'new' liberalism that emerged at the turn of the twentieth century, but they are principles most associated with socialism. Moreover, the nature of a viable animal welfarism emerging from a more enlightened anthropocentrism will have to be worked out in detail. The key questions are, firstly, what human benefits are to be regarded as sufficiently important to warrant the infliction of suffering of animals, and, secondly, what would this mean for the moral legitimacy of present ways in which animals are exploited?

The problem of agency

Although there have been concerted attempts to justify according to animals a higher moral status than allowed for by the moral orthodoxy, these remain, with the exception of ecology, peripheral to the ideologies from which they are derived. The conventional position, in the West at least, remains that, whilst having important interests, animals are inferior morally to humans. The dominance of anthropocentrism in ideological discourse is a reminder of the fact that ideologies are a reflection of power structures in society and, in this case, the pre-eminence of human beings (Freeden, 1998: 22–3). To give an example, the class basis of liberalism and socialism has given ground in the post-1945 period to a feminism which has arisen on the back of an emerging women's movement, and an environmentalism which has been a product of factors such as affluence and the creation of a new class more likely to have post-material values.

The attachment of social groups to particular ideologies reveals a crucial problem for those who want better protection of animal interests. The problem for animals is that, as Adams (1993: 292) points out, 'the "oppressed group" is not going to have its consciousness raised or participate in its own liberation'. Moreover, for humans to campaign on behalf of them requires an altruism that is much more profound than for other social movements. Not only does it involve action to seek the advancement of the interests of another species, there is also a potential conflict between the interests of animals and those of humans. Animals provide direct economic benefits: they are used as a source of nutrition, as vehicles to test potentially dangerous products, as scientific models in the search for new drug products and medical procedures, as well as sources of entertainment and clothing.

Animal rights or liberation, then, remains a potent threat to human interests, and anthropocentrism is a powerful creed with a vested interest intent, for the most part, in maintaining species domination. There are some areas where human and animal interests may coincide, the human – environmental and food safety – consequences of factory farming being a classic example. Such cases provide an unsatisfactory basis for the protection of animal interests because they are contingent upon also being in the interests of humans. As we have seen, there are many occasions where this is not the case.

A necessary, although not sufficient, condition for the significant improvement of the well-being of animals is that their interests be incorporated fully into mainstream political theory and practice. However, achieving this goal remains elusive. This is particularly the case for liberalism, where there is no obvious significant human agency, other than the tiny minority of the population who campaign for reforms to the ways that animals are treated. Despite their weaknesses from an animal protection perspective, the attraction of socialist and feminist attempts to incorporate animal interests, on the other hand, is that they ally animals with exploited, and numerically significant, *human* groups. There is little evidence, however, that at the level of praxis the theoretical case for incorporation has been accepted by anything more than a small proportion of feminists and socialists. It remains an open question whether this can change. In the meantime, focusing on well-known and respected liberal concepts such as rights, freedom, individualism, universalism and equality, embellished, as suggested, with some of the insights of the other ideologies considered, would seem to offer, despite the problems identified in this book, the best hope for advancements in animal well-being.

Bibliography

Ackerman, B. (1980) *Social Justice in the Liberal State*, New Haven: Yale University Press.

Adams, C. (1990) *The Sexual Politics of Meat: A Feminist Vegetarian Critical Theory*, New York: Polity.

Adams, C. (1993) 'The Feminist Traffic in Animals', in G. Gaard, *Ecofeminism: Women, Animals, Nature*, Philadelphia: Temple University Press: 195–218.

Adams, C. (1994) Neither *Man Nor Beast: Feminism and the Defence of Animals*, New York: Continuum.

Adams, C. (1995) 'Women-Battering and Harm to Animals', in C. Adams and J. Donovan, *Animals and Women: Feminist Theoretical Explorations*, Durham, N.C.: Duke University Press: 55–84.

Adams, C. (1996) 'Caring About Suffering: A Feminist Exploration', in J. Donovan and C. Adams, *Beyond Animal Rights: A Feminist Caring Ethic for the Treatment of Animals*, New York: Continuum: 170–96.

Adams, C. and J. Donovan (eds) (1995) *Animals and Women: Feminist Theoretical Explorations*, Durham, N.C.: Duke University Press.

Adams, I. (1993) *Political Ideology Today*, Manchester: Manchester University Press.

Aitkenhead, D. (2003) 'The Slaughterhouse Rules', *Guardian*, 14 September.

Arblaster, A. (1984) *The Rise and Decline of Western Liberalism*, Oxford: Basil Blackwell.

Arneson, R. (2000) 'The Priority of the Right Over the Good Rides Again', in P. Kelly (ed.), *Impartiality, Neutrality and Justice: Re-reading Brian Barry's Justice as Impartiality*, Edinburgh: Edinburgh University Press: 60–86.

Attfield, R. (2003) *Environmental Ethics*, Cambridge: Polity.

Avineri, S. and A. De-Shalt (eds) (1992) *Communitarianism and Individualism*, Oxford: Oxford University Press.

Barry, B. (1989) *Theories of Justice*, Hemel Hempstead: Harvester-Wheatsheaf.

Barry, B. (1995) *Justice as Impartiality*, Oxford: Clarendon Press.

Barry, B. (1999) 'Sustainability and Intergenerational Justice', in A. Dobson (ed.), *Fairness and Futurity: Essays on Environmental Sustainability and Social Justice*. Oxford: Oxford University Press, 93–117.

Barry, B. (2001) *Culture and Equality: An Egalitarian Critique of Multi-culturalism*, Cambridge: Polity.

Barry, J. (1999) *Rethinking Green Politics: Nature, Virtue and Progress*, London: Sage.

Barry, N. (2000) *An Introduction to Modern Political Theory* (fourth edition), Basingstoke: Macmillan.

Baum, B. (1997) 'Feminism, Liberalism and Cultural Pluralism: J. S. Mill on Mormon Polygamy', *The Journal of Political Philosophy*, 5, 3: 230–53.

Beiner, R. (1992) *What's the Matter with Liberalism?*, Berkeley: University of California Press.

Bellamy, R. (1992) *Liberalism and Modern Society: An Historical Argument*, Cambridge: Polity Press.

Bentham, J. (1948) *An Introduction to the Principles of Morals and Legislation*, New York: Hafner Press.

Benton, T. (1993) *Natural Relations: Ecology, Social Justice and Animal Rights*, London: Verso.

Benton, T. (1993a) 'Animal Rights and Social Relations', in A. Dobson and P. Lucardie (eds), *The Politics of Nature: Explorations in Green Political Thought*, London: Routledge: 161–76.

Benton, T. (1996) 'Animal Rights: An Eco-Socialist View', in R. Garner (ed.), *Animal Rights: The Changing Debate*, New York: New York University Press: 19–41.

Benton, T. and R. Redfearn (1996) 'The Politics of Animal Rights: Where is the Left?', *New Left Review*, 215: 43–58.

Boardman, R. (1981) *International Organisations and the Conservation of Nature*, London: Macmillan.

Bramwell, A. (1989) *Ecology in the Twentieth Century*, New Haven: Yale University Press.

Brown, C. (1998) 'International Social Justice', in D. Boucher and P. Kelly (eds), *Social Justice: From Hume to Walzer*, London: Routledge: 102–19.

Callicott, J. (1995) 'Animal Liberation: A Triangular Affair', in R. Elliot (ed.), *Environmental Ethics*, Oxford: Oxford University Press: 29–59.

Callicott, J. (1992) 'Animal Liberation and Environmental Ethics: Back Together Again', in E. Hargrove (ed.), *The Animal Rights: Environmental Ethics Debate*, Albany: State University of New York Press: 249–61.

Caney, S. (1992) 'Liberalism and Communitarianism: A Misconceived Debate', *Political Studies*, 40, 2: 273–89.

Carruthers, P. (1992) *The Animals Issue*, Cambridge: Cambridge University Press.

Cavalieri, P. and Singer, P. (eds) (1993) *The Great Ape Project: Equality beyond humanity*, London: Fourth Estate.

Clark, S. (1984) *The Moral Status of Animals*, Oxford: Clarendon Press.

Clark, S. (1987) 'Animals, Ecosystems and the Liberal Ethic', *The Monist*, 79, 3: 114–33.

Clarke, P. and Linzey, A. (1990) *Political Theory and Animal Rights*. London: Pluto Press.

Craig (1990) *British General Election Manifestos 1959–87*, Aldershot, Gower.

Crowder, G. (1994) 'Pluralism and Liberalism', *Political Studies*, 42, 2: 293–305.

Darwell, S. (1998) *Philosophical Ethics*, Boulder, CO.: Westview Press.

DeGrazia, D. (1996) *Taking Animals Seriously: Mental Life and Moral Status*, Cambridge: Cambridge University Press.

DeGrazia, D. (2002) *Animal Rights: A Very Short Introduction*, Oxford: Oxford University Press.

Descartes, R. (1912) 'Discourse V', in J. Veitch (ed.), *René Descartes: A Discourse on Method*, London: Dent: 90–7.

Dobson, A. (1998) *Justice and the Environment*. Oxford: Oxford University Press.

Dobson, A. (2000) *Green Political Thought* (third edition), London: Unwin Hyman.

Donovan, J. (1993) 'Animal Rights and Feminist Theory', in G. Gaard, *Ecofeminism: Women, Animals, Nature*, Philadelphia: Temple University Press: 167–94.

Donovan, J. (1996) 'Animal Rights and Feminist Theory', in J. Donovan and C. Adams (eds), *Beyond Animal Rights: A Feminist Caring Ethic for the Treatment of Animals*, New York: Continuum: 34–59.

Donovan, J. and C. Adams (eds) (1996) *Beyond Animal Rights: A Feminist Caring Ethic for the Treatment of Animals*, New York: Continuum.

Dunayer, J. (1995) 'Sexist Words, Speciesist Roots', in C. Adams and J. Donovan, *Animals and Women: Feminist Theoretical Explanations*, Durham, N.C.: Duke University Press: 11–31.

Dworkin, R. (1975) 'The Original Position', in N. Daniels (ed.), *Reading Rawls: Critical Studies of A Theory of Justice*, Oxford: Basil Blackwell: 16–53.

Dworkin, R. (1978) 'Liberalism', in S. Hampshire (ed.), *Public and Private Morality*, Cambridge: Cambridge University Press: 113–43.

Dworkin, R. (1996) *Freedom's Law: The Moral Reading of the American Constitution*, Oxford: Oxford University Press.

Eckersley, R. (1992) *Environmentalism and Political Theory*, London: UCL.

Elliot, R. (1984) 'Rawlsian Justice and non-Human Animals', *Journal of Applied Philosophy*, 1: 95–106.

Elston, M. (1990) 'Women and Anti-Vivisection in Victorian England', in N. Rupke (ed.), *Vivisection in Historical Perspective*, London: Routledge: 259–94.

Etzioni, A. (ed.) (1995) *New Communitarian Thinking: Persons, Virtues, Institutions, and Communities*, Charlottesville: University Press of Virginia.

Etzioni, A. (1999) 'Debate: The Good Society', *Journal of Political Philosophy*, 7, 1: 88–103.

Favre, D. and V. Tsang (1993) 'The Development of Anti-Cruelty Laws During the 1800s', *Detroit College of Law Review*, 1: 1–33.

FAWC (1985) *Report on the Welfare of Livestock When Slaughtered by Religious Methods*, London: HMSO.

FAWC (2003) *Report on the Welfare of Farmed Animals at Slaughter or Killing*, London: HMSO.

Ferguson, M. (1998) *Animal Advocacy and Englishwomen, 1780–1900: Patriots, Nation, and Empire*, Ann Arbor: University of Michigan Press.

Finsen, L. and Finsen, S. (1994) *The Animal Rights Movement in American: From Compassion to Respect*, New York: Twayne.

Foster, P. (1995) *Women and the Health Care Industry: An Unhealthy Relationship?*, Buckingham: Open University Press.

Fox, W. (1995) *Towards a Transpersonal Ecology*, Totnes: Resurgence.

Francione, G. (1995) *Animals, Property and the Law*, Philadelphia: Temple University Press.

Francione, G. (1995a) 'Abortion and Animal Rights: Are They Compatible Issues?', in C. Adams and J. Donovan (eds), *Animals and Women: Feminist Theoretical Explanations*, Durham, N.C.: Duke University Press: 149–59.

Francione, G. (1996) *Rain Without Thunder: The Ideology of the Animal Rights Movement*, Philadelphia: Temple University Press.

Francione, G. (2000) *Introduction to Animal Rights: Your Child or the Dog*, Philadelphia: Temple University Press.

Fraser, A. and D. Broom (1990) *Farm Animal Behaviour and Welfare*, Wallingford: Cabi Publishing.

Freeden, M. (1998) *Ideologies and Political Theory: A Conceptual Approach*, Oxford: Clarendon Press.

French, R. (1975) *Antivivisection and Medical Science in Victorian Society*, Princeton: Princeton University Press.

Frey, R. (1980) *Interests and Rights: The Case Against Animals*, Oxford: Oxford University Press.

Frey, R. (1983) *Rights, Killing and Suffering*, Oxford: Clarendon Press.

Frey, R. (1987) 'Autonomy and the Value of Animal Life', *Monist*, 70.

Frey, R. (2002) 'Ethics, Animals and Scientific Inquiry', in Gluck, *et al.*, *Applied Ethics in Animal Research*, Indiana: Purdue University Press: 13–24.

Gaard, G. (ed.) (1993) *Ecofeminism: Women, Animals, Nature*, Philadelphia: Temple University Press.

Gaard, G. (1993a) 'Living Interconnections with Animals and Nature', in G. Gaard, *Ecofeminism: Women, Animals, Nature*, Philadelphia: Temple University Press: 1–12.

Galston, W. (1980) *Justice and the Human Good*, Chicago: University of Chicago Press.

Galston, W. (1982) 'Defending Liberalism', *American Political Science Review*, 76: 621–9.

Garner, R. (1993) *Animals, Politics and Morality*, Manchester: Manchester University Press.

Garner, R. (1998) *Political Animals: Animal Protection Politics in Britain and the United States*, Basingstoke: Macmillan.

Garner, R. (1999) 'Animal Protection and Legislators in Britain and the United States', *Journal of Legislative Studies*, 5, 2: 92–114.

Garner, R. (2000) 'The Scope of Green Realism', *Contemporary Politics*, 6, 2: 185–90.

Gilligan, C. (1982) *In a Different Voice*, Cambridge, MA: Harvard University Press.

Gluck, J., T. Di Pasquale and F. Orlans (2002) *Applied Ethics in Animal Research*, Indiana: Purdue University Press.

Goodin, R. (1992) 'The High Ground is Green', *Environmental Politics*, 1, 1: 1–8.

Goodin, R. and A. Reeve (eds) (1989) *Liberal Neutrality*, London: Routledge.

Goodpaster, K. (1978) 'On Being Morally Considerable', *Journal of Philosophy*, 75: 308–25.

Gray, J. (1997) *Endgames: Questions in Late Modern Political Thought*, Cambridge: Polity.

Gray, J. (2002) *Straw Dogs: Thoughts on Humans and Other Animals*, London: Granta.

Greanville, P. and D. Moss (1985) 'The Emerging Face of the Movement', *Animals' Agenda*, March–April: 36.

Griffin, D. (1992) *Animal Minds*, Chicago: University of Chicago Press.

Griffin, S. (1978) *Woman and Nature: The Roaring Inside Her*, New York: Harper & Rowe.

Gruen, L. (1993) 'Dismantling Oppression. An Analysis of the Connection Between Women and Animals', in G. Gaard, *Ecofeminism: Women, Animals, Nature*, Philadelphia: Temple University Press, 60–90.

Hay, P. (1988) 'Ecological Values and Western Political Traditions: From Anarchism to Fascism', *Politics*, 8, 2: 22–9.

Hamilton, M. (1987) 'The Elements of the Concept of Ideology', *Political Studies*, 35, 1: 18–38.

Hargrove, E. (ed.) (1992) *The Animal Rights/Environmental Ethics Debate*, Albany: State University of New York Press.

Harrison, G. (1979) 'Relativism and Tolerance', in P. Laslett and J. Fishkin (eds), *Philosophy, Politics and Society*, Fifth Series, Oxford: Basil Blackwell: 273–90.

Hayward, T. (1995) *Ecological Thought: An Introduction*, Cambridge: Polity.

Hayward, T. (1998) *Political Theory and Ecological Values*, Cambridge: Polity.

Hayward, T. (2000) 'Constitutional Environmental Rights: A Case for Political Analysis', *Political Studies*, 48, 3: 558–72.

Hobbes, T. (1992) *Leviathan*, Cambridge: Cambridge University Press.

Holland, A. (1984) 'On Behalf of a Moderate Speciesism', *Journal of Applied Philosophy*, 1, 2: 281–91.

Husak, D. (2000) 'Liberal Neutrality, Autonomy and Drug Prohibitions', *Philosophy and Public Affairs*, 29, 1: 43–80.

Jahme, C. (2000) *Beauty and the Beasts: Women, Ape and Evolution*, London: Virago.

Jamieson, D. (1998) 'Animal Liberation is an Environmental Ethic', *Environmental Values*, 7: 41–57.

Jasper, J. and Nelkin, D. (1992) *The Animal Rights Crusade: The Growth of a Moral Protest*, New York: Free Press.

Johnson, A. (1991) *Factory Farming*, Oxford: Blackwell.

Johnson, E. (1976) *Species and Morality*, Unpublished PhD thesis, Princeton University.

Johnson, L. (1991) *A Morally Deep World*, Cambridge: Cambridge University Press.

Kant, I. (1965) *Metaphysics of Morals*, New York: Bobbs Merrill.

Kean, H. (1998) *Animal rights: Political and Social Change in Britain Since 1800*, London: Reaktion Books.

Kelch, T. (1998) 'Toward a Non-Property Status for Animals', *New York University Environmental Law Journal*, 6, 3: 531–85.

Kheel, M. (1996) 'The Liberation of Nature: A Circular Affair', in J. Donovan and C. Adams, *Beyond Animal Rights: A Feminist Caring Ethic for the Treatment of Animals*, New York: Continuum: 17–33.

Kukathas, C. and P. Pettit (1990) *Rawls: A Theory of Justice and its Critics*, Cambridge: Polity Press.

Kymlicka, W. (1989) 'Liberal Individualism and Liberal Neutrality', *Ethics*, 99: 883–905.

Kymlicka, W. (1990) *Contemporary Political Philosophy: An Introduction*, Oxford: Oxford University Press.

Lansbury, C. (1985) *The Old Brown Dog: Women, Workers, and Vivisection in Edwardian England*, Madison: University of Wisconsin Press.

Larmore, C. (1999) 'The Moral basis of Political Liberalism', *Journal of Philosophy*, 96, 12: 599–625.

Leahy, M. (1991) *Against Liberation: Putting Animals into Perspective*, London: Routledge.

Leopold, A. (1949) *A Sand County Almanac*, Oxford: Oxford University Press.

Locke, J. (1988) *Two Treatises of Government*, Cambridge: Cambridge University Press.

Luke, B. (1995) 'Taming Ourselves or Going Feral? Toward a Nonpatriarchal Metaethic of Animal Liberation', in C. Adams and J. Donovan (eds), *Animals and Women: Feminist Theoretical Explorations*, Durham, N.C.: Duke University Press: 290–319.

Luke, B. (1996) 'Justice, Caring and Animal Liberation', in Donovan and Adams, *Beyond Animal Rights*: 77–102.

Lukes, S. (1985) *Marxism and Morality*, Oxford: Clarendon Press.

Lyster, S. (1985) *International Wildlife Law*, Cambridge: Grotius.

MacIntyre, A. (1985) *After Virtue: A Study in Moral Theory* (second edition), London: Duckworth.

MacIntyre, A. (1988) *Whose Justice? Which Rationality?*, London: Duckworth.

MacIntyre, A. (1999) *Dependent Rational Animals: Why Human Beings Need the Virtues*, London: Duckworth.

Manning, R. (1996) 'Caring for Animals', in J. Donovan and C. Adams (eds), *Beyond Animal Rights: A Feminist Caring Ethic for the Treatment of Animals*, New York: Continuum: 103–25.

Mason, J. (2002) 'Making a Killing: The Power and Influence of Animal Agriculture in America', in K. Stallwood (ed.), *A Primer on Animal Rights*, New York: Lantern Books: 199–209.

Mason, J. and P. Singer (1990) *Animal Factories*, New York: Harmony Books.

Matthews, F. (1991) *The Ecological Self*, London: Routledge.

McCloskey, H. (1979) 'Moral Rights and Animals', *Inquiry*, 22: 23–54.

Midgley, M. (1983) *Animals and Why They Matter*, Harmondsworth: Penguin.

Mill, J. S. (1969) 'Three Essays on Religion', in J. M. Robson (ed.), *John Stuart Mill: Essays on Ethics, Religion and Society*, London: Routledge and Kegan Paul: 10–122.

Mill, J. S. (1972) *Utilitarianism, On Liberty, and Considerations on Representative Government*, London: Dent.

Miller, D. (1976) *Social Justice*, Oxford: Clarendon Press.

Mills, S. and P. Williams (1986) 'Political Animals', *Marxism Today*, April: 30–3.

Morton, D. (1989) 'The Animals (Scientific Procedures) Act 1986', in D. Blackman, P. Humphreys and P. Todd (eds), *Animal Welfare and the Law*, Cambridge: Cambridge University Press: 195–219.

Mulhall, S. and A. Swift (1992) *Liberals and Communitarians*, Oxford: Blackwell.

Moller Okin, S. (1993) 'Review of *Political Liberalism*', *Political Theory*, 87, 4: 1010–11.

Naess, A. (1973) 'The Shallow and the Deep, Long Range Ecology Movement. A Summary', *Inquiry*, 16: 95–100.

Nagel, T. (1987) 'Moral Conflict and Political Legitimacy', *Philosophy and Public Affairs*, 16, 3: 215–40.

Narveson, J. (1977) 'Animal Rights', *Canadian Journal of Philosophy*, 7: 161–78.

Narveson, J. (1987) 'On a Case for Animal Rights', *Monist*, 70: 30–47.

Neal, P. (1997) *Liberalism and its Discontents*, London: Macmillan.

Nibert, D. (1994) 'Animal Rights and Human Social Issues', *Society and Animals*, 2, 2: 115–24.

Norton, B. (1991) *Toward Unity Among Environmentalists*, Oxford: Oxford University Press.

Noske, B. (1989) *Humans and Other Animals. Beyond the Boundaries of Anthropology*, London: Pluto.

Nozick, R. (1974) *Anarchy, State and Utopia*, Oxford: Basil Blackwell.

Opotow, S. (1993) 'Animals and the Scope of Justice', *Journal of Social Issues*, 49, 1: 71–85.

Passmore, J. (1974) *Man's Responsibility for Nature*, London: Duckworth.

Pluhar, E. (1995) *Beyond Prejudice: The Moral Significance of Human and Nonhuman Animals*, Durham: Duke University Press.

Plant, R. (1991) *Modern Political Thought*, Oxford: Basil Blackwell.

Porritt, J. and Winner, D. (1988) *The Coming of the Greens*, London: Fontana.

Poulter, S. (1998) *Ethnicity, Law and Human Rights: The English Experience*, Oxford: Clarendon Press.

Pritchard, M. and Robinson, W. (1981) 'Justice and the Treatment of Animals: A Critique of Rawls', *Environmental Ethics*, 3: 55–61.

Radford, M. (1996) 'Partial Protection: Animal Welfare and the Law', in R. Garner (ed.), *Animal Rights: The Changing Debate*, New York: New York University Press: 67–91.

Radford, M. (1999) ' "Unnecessary Suffering": The Cornerstone of Animal Protection Legislation Considered', *Criminal Law Review*, September: 702–13.

Radford, M. (2001) *Animal Welfare Law in Britain*, Oxford: Oxford University Press.

Rawls, J. (1963) 'The Sense of Justice', *The Philosophical Review*, 122: 281–305.

Rawls, J. (1972) *A Theory of Justice*, Oxford: Oxford University Press.

Rawls, J. (1991) 'Justice as Fairness: Political Not Metaphysical', in J. Angelo Corlett (ed.), *Equality and Liberty: Analysing Rawls and Nozick*, Basingstoke: Macmillan: 145–73.

Rawls, J. (1993) *Political Liberalism*, New York: Columbia University Press.

Raz, J. (1986) *The Morality of Freedom*, Oxford: Clarendon Press.

Regan, T. (1984) *The Case for Animal Rights*, London: Routledge.

Regan, T. (1987) *The Struggle for Animal Rights*, Clark's Summit, PA: International Society for Animal Rights.

Regan, T. (1991) *The Thee Generation: Reflections on the Coming Revolution*, Philadelphia: Temple University Press.

Regan, T. and P. Singer (1989) *Animal Rights and Human Obligations* (second edition), Englewood Cliffs, NJ: Prentice Hall.

Richards, D. (1971) *A Theory of Reasons for Action*, Oxford: Clarendon Press.

Rifkin, J. (1992) *Beyond Beef: The Rise and Fall of the Cattle Culture*, Harmondsworth: Penguin.

Roberts, A. (2002) 'The Trade in Drugs and Wildlife', in K. Stallwood (ed.), *A Primer on Animal Rights*, New York: Lantern Books: 45–9.

Rodd, R. (1990) *Biology, Ethics and Animals*, Oxford: Clarendon Press.

Rodman, J. (1993) 'Four Forms of Ecological Consciousness Reconsidered', in D. Scherer and T. Attig (eds), *Ethics and the Environment*, Englewood Cliffs, N.J.: Prentice-Hall: 82–92.

Rollin, B. (1981) *Animal Rights and Human Morality*, New York: Prometheus.

Rollin, B. (1995) *The Frankenstein Syndrome*, Cambridge: Cambridge University Press.

Roth, A. (1988) *Parliamentary Profiles*, London.

Rowan, A. (1989) 'The development of the animal protection movement', *Journal of NIH Research*, November–December: 97–100.

Rowlands, M. (1998) *Animal Rights: A Philosophical Defence*, Basingstoke: Macmillan.

Rowlands, M. (2002) *Animals Like Us*, London: Verso

Ryder, R. (1975) *Victims of Science*, London: Davis-Poynter.

Ryder, R. (1989) *Animal Revolution: Changing Attitudes Towards Speciesism*, Oxford: Basil Blackwell.

Ryder, R. (2000) *Animal Revolution: Changing Attitudes Towards Speciesism* (second edition), Oxford: Berg.

Salt, H. (1980) *Animals' Rights Considered in Relation to Social Progress* (originally published in 1892), London: Fontwell.

Sandel, M. (ed.) (1984) *Liberalism and its Critics*, Oxford: Basil Blackwell.

Sandel, M. (1998) *Liberalism and the Limits of Justice* (second edition), Cambridge: Cambridge University Press.

Sapontzis, S. (1987) *Morals, Reason, and Animals*, Philadelphia: Temple University Press.

Scruton, R. (2000) *Animal Rights and Wrongs*, London: Metro.

Scully, M. (2002) *Dominion: The Power of Man, the Suffering of Animals and the Call to Mercy*, New York: St. Martin's Press.

Sharpe, R. (1988) *The Cruel Deception: The Use of Animals in Medical Research*, Wellingborough: Thorsons.

Sher, G. (1997) *Beyond Neutrality: Perfectionism and Politics*, Cambridge: Cambridge University Press.

Singer, B. (1988) 'An Extension of Rawls' Theory of Justice to Environmental Ethics', *Environmental Ethics*, 10: 213–32.

Singer, P. (1979) 'Killing Humans and Killing Animals', *Inquiry*, 22: 145–56.

Singer, P. (1981) *The Expanding Circle: Ethics and Sociobiology*, Oxford: Oxford University Press.

Singer, P. (1990) *Animal Liberation* (second edition), London: Cape.

Sinopoli, P. (1993) 'Liberalism and Contested Conceptions of the Good: The Limits of Neutrality', *The Journal of Politics*, 55, 3: 644–63.

Spencer, C. (1995) *The Heretic's Feast: A History of Vegetarianism*, Hanover: University Press of New England.

Sperling, S. (1988) *Animal Liberators: Research and Morality*, Berkeley: University of California Press.

Spiegel, M. (1988) *The Dreaded Comparison: Humans and Animal Slavery*, New York: Mirror Books.

Squires, J. (1999) *Gender in Political Theory*, Cambridge: Polity Press.

Stallwood, K. (2002) *A Primer on Animal Rights*, New York: Lantern Books.

Sweeney, N. (1990) *Animals and Cruelty and Law*, Bristol: Alibi.

Tam, H. (1998) *Communitarianism: A New Agenda for Politics and Citizenship*, Basingstoke: Macmillan.

Tannenbaum, J. (1995) 'Animals and the Law: Property, Cruelty, Rights', *Social Research*, 62: 125–93.

Taylor, C. (1979) *Hegel and Modern Society*, Cambridge: Cambridge University Press.

Taylor, C. (1984) 'Hegel: History and Politics', in M. Sandel (ed.), *Liberalism and its Critics*, Oxford: Basil Blackwell: 121–38.

Taylor, P. W. (1986) *Respect for Nature: A Theory of Environmental Ethics*, Princeton: Princeton University Press.

Tester, K. (1991) *Animals and Society: The Humanity of Animal Rights*, London: Routledge

Thero, D. (1995) 'Rawls and Environmental Ethics: A Critical Examination of the Literature', *Environmental Ethics*, 17, 93–106.

Thomas, R. (1983) *The Politics of Hunting*, Aldershot: Gower.

Thompson, J. (1990) 'A Refutation of Environmental Ethics', *Environmental Ethics*, 12: 147–60.

Tong, R. (1998) *Feminist thought: A More Comprehensive Introduction* (second edition), Boulder, CO: Westview.

Townsend, A. (1976) 'Radical Vegetarians', *Australasian Journal of Philosophy*, 57: 85–93.

Vandeveer, D. (1979) 'Of Beasts, Persons and the Original Position', *Monist*, 62, 3: 368–77.

Varner, G. (1998) *In Nature's Interests? Animal Rights and Environmental Ethics*, New York: Oxford University Press.

Vincent, A. (1995) *Modern Political Ideologies*, Oxford: Blackwell.

Waldron, J. (ed.) (1987) *'Nonsense Upon Stilts: Bentham, Burke and Marx on the Rights of Man*, London: Methuen.

Waldron, J. (1989) 'Legislation and Moral Neutrality', in R. Goodin and A. Reeve (eds), *Liberal Neutrality*, London: Routledge: 61–83.

Walzer, M. (1983) *Spheres of Justice: A Defence of Pluralism and Equality*, Oxford: Blackwell.

Walzer, M. (1990) 'The Communitarian Critique of Liberalism', *Political Theory*, 18, 1: 6–23.

Walzer, M. (1992) 'Membership', in S. Avineri and A. De-Shalt, *Communitarianism and Individualism*, Oxford: Oxford University Press: 65–84.

Watkins, K. (1999) 'An Examination of Women's Involvement in Contemporary Campaigns Around Animal Welfare and Animal Rights', *University of Manchester Sociology Working Papers*, 16: 1–24.

Wenz, P. (1988) *Environmental Justice*, Albany: State University of New York Press.

Wicklund (1997) 'Abrogating Property Status in the Fight for Animal Rights', *The Yale Law Journal*, 107: 569–74.

Wise, S. (2000) *Rattling the Cage: Toward Legal Rights to Animals*, Cambridge, MA: Perseus Books.

Wissenburg, M. (1993) 'The Idea of Nature and the Nature of Distributive Justice', in A. Dobson and P. Lucardie (eds), *The Politics of Nature: Explorations in Green Political Thought*, London: Routledge: 3–20.

Wissenburg, M. (1998) *Green Liberalism: The Free and the Green Society*, London: UCL Press.

Wissenburg, M. (1999) 'An Extension of the Rawlsian Savings Principle to Liberal Theories of Justice in General', in A. Dobson (ed.), *Fairness and Futurity: Essays on Environmental Sustainability and Social Justice*, Oxford: Oxford University Press: 173–98.

Wolfson, D. (1996) *Beyond the Law: Agribusiness and the systemic Abuse of Animals Raised for Food or Food Production*, New York: Archimedian Press.

Young, H. (1999) 'The Intolerant in Pursuit of Political Correctness', *Guardian*, 13 July.

Index